Selly Park and Beyond

*The Story of Geneviève Dupuis and the Congregation
of the Sisters of Charity of St. Paul the Apostle*

by

J. J. Scarisbrick

Emeritus Professor of History University of Warwick

Published by the Sisters of Charity of St. Paul the Apostle
to celebrate the 150th Anniversary of the Foundation of the Congregation
Copyright © 1997

ISBN 0 9530007 0 2

Acknowledgements

Sister Maria Rosa: for agreeing to write the Foreword. Sister Anne Cunningham: Research and Archive Material. Sister Ann Connolly: Photographs and Book Jacket Illustrations.

Many of the illustrations used in this publication have been taken from the archives and credits have not been made possible. The publishers however acknowledge with gratitude the numerous photographs given to the Congregation by so many friends, and trust that no offence will be caused with the use of such historical material.

Produced by Joseph E. Durham, Heritage and Education 01782 623431
Designed by: Henryk Szor Associates Ecclesiastical Design
Printed and bound in England by Print Partnership

Contents

The Beginnings 1

The Twentieth Century 33

The Voice of Geneviève Dupuis 55

Superiors General 57

Sisters Reminisce 59

Branch Houses 65

Appendices 87

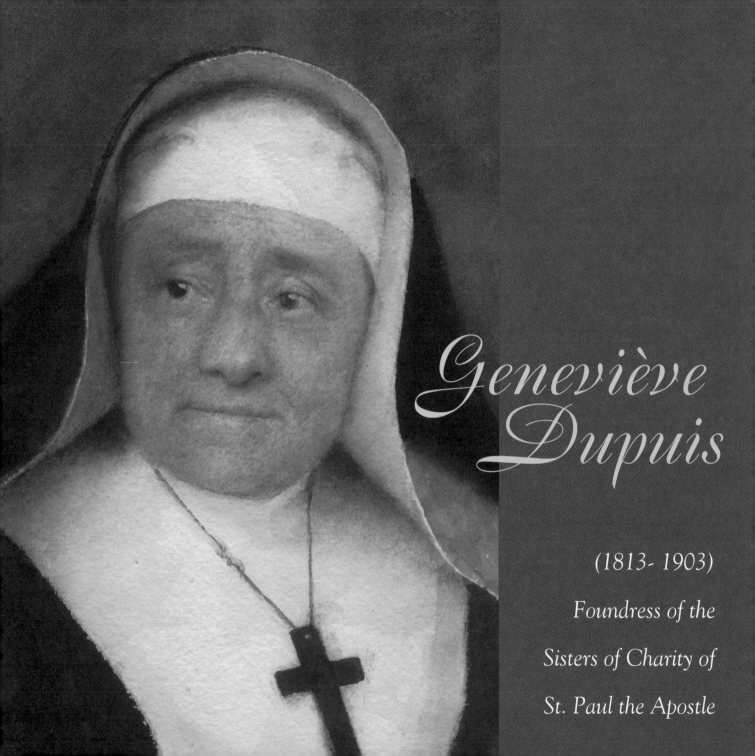

Geneviève Dupuis

(1813- 1903)

Foundress of the

Sisters of Charity of

St. Paul the Apostle

The story of our Congregation is a tapestry of many strands, colours of many shades and hues, a story of rich blessings, and not a few trials, disappointments and contradictions. It is the story of courageous women whose journey in faith never wavered and who lived a deep relationship with Christ in the midst of the ordinary and common place. These were strong and gentle women who felt at home in the parochial scene and were sensitive to the hardships and struggles of people for whom the Kingdom was no strange land, at least in their prayers and dreams.

Our story line is a varied one. While the cultural milieu has changed enormously since the England of Mother Geneviève's day, the need for values and attitudes worthy of the dignity of the human person is no less apparent. Therein lies the challenge for our onward journey.

In this decade of Evangelisation and on the threshold of the Third Millennium, we feel called both individually and as a Congregation to ensure that our commitment to love and service flows from an evangelical heart.

Over the past one hundred and fifty years our methods and customs have changed to suit the needs of the people in different eras and in different countries. However, living in close relationship with Christ in a total commitment, "leaving everything behind in order to live at his side" *(Vita Consecrata)*, is the dimension of our lives that can never be replaced nor diminished.

"Behold I am with you always even to the end of time", promises Jesus. Inherent in that promise are the wisdom and grace that will never be wanting to us as long as we operate from that source.

In the realm of the spiritual the journey is always only beginning; newness is dear to the Spirit as is the joy of surprises. That Spirit of Christ which bonds us all across the mixed terrain of one hundred and fifty years in a shared charism will continue to lead us towards tomorrow's promised land. The journey, though, will be decidedly different in form and expression, marked by a creative fidelity consonant with the needs of tomorrow's world. However, the essentials will be unchanged:

a vowed life committed to love in a faith-relationship with Christ;

a task, a mission embraced in the spirit of the beatitudes;

a corporate story that will be simply a continuation of our Congregational gospel;

the good news of our charism at the service of the Kingdom.

Sr. Maria Rosa O'Sullivan
Superior General
3rd January 1997

The Beginnings

Between the Catholic Emancipation Act of 1829, which ended generations of penal repression of the old Faith in Britain, and the Second Vatican Council in the 1960s, English Catholicism flowered in a remarkable way.

Emancipation was followed by restoration of a fully-fledged hierarchy in 1850. Then the 'Second Spring' witnessed a momentous and continuing influx into the Church of converts from Anglicanism, and from 1840 onwards came a flood of thousands of Irish immigrants, fleeing famine and poverty at home, and searching for employment, often in appalling conditions, on the railways and in shipyards and factories of industrial Britain. By 1800 shrunken English Catholicism had become a largely rural, marginalised sect - widely tolerated precisely because it was unthreatening. A hundred years later it had burgeoned into a thriving, highly structured and largely urban, national Church. Served by zealous bishops and clergy, ultramontane and increasingly self-confident, the English Catholics spoke about and prayed openly for the conversion of England and the full restoration of the Faith of their fathers, a goal which many believed to be in their reach.

All this required and in turn made possible a building programme of which any community would have been proud, but which was an astonishing achievement for one whose members were mainly drawn from the urban proletariat: hundreds of churches and chapels and presbyteries, and a score of cathedrals; hundreds of schools and colleges; seminaries, orphanages and infirmaries; numerous buildings bought or built to house monks, friars and several dozen new male religious orders; hundreds of nunneries.

❧

There had been nuns in medieval England, of course: some 70 communities on the eve of the Reformation, including half a dozen houses of men and women belonging to England's only native order, the Gilbertines, and one large 'double' community of Bridgettines at Isleworth in Middlesex. All were scattered and their buildings and land seized in the 1530s, except for a female Bridgettine community, which survived heroically in exile for 200 years and is still in existence. Within a few decades of the final victory of the Reformation, however, English women were making their way to the Continent to pursue the religious life whether in existing houses of Benedictine, Franciscan or other nuns, or to found their own houses of those traditional orders. By 1642 seventeen such exiled communities had been established.

Meanwhile there had appeared among these exiles the astonishing Mary Ward, who, despite daunting opposition from the authorities, had eventually succeeded in establishing the Institute of the Blessed Virgin Mary and thus founding the first-ever English order of nuns (albeit on foreign soil).

Mary Ward's venture was part of a larger phenomenon. The sixteenth and seventeenth centuries, first in Italy and then most notably France, saw the emergence of scores of new female religious congregations. Indeed, it was during this time that female religious came to play the major role in the life of the Church which they retained until recently. The new orders were different from those which had gone before because they were dedicated to good works, that is, the active life rather than the contemplative, and therefore to a life that was in the world, rather than enclosed. Like many of their new counterparts, the new-style sisters of the Catholic Reformation gave their lives to serving the poor, the sick and the dying, the orphaned and insane, the lost and the illiterate. Nursing, and increasingly teaching, were at the heart of their apostolate.

These developments on the Continent had inevitably had little effect on the life of the beleaguered Catholic community in England, though an illicit IBVM convent school had been opened in York in the 1690s and there was another house in Hammersmith. By the early nineteenth century the English communities of Canonesses of St

Augustine, Dominicanesses, Poor Clare and Benedictine sisters had returned home from the Continent and were running nine schools. Their numbers had been enlarged by a handful of French communities who had fled the Revolution and put down permanent roots in English soil.

From the mid-1830s, however, the growth of female religious life in England quickened dramatically. There were important new arrivals from Ireland (especially the Sisters of Mercy, who came to Bermondsey in 1839) and from France and then from Belgium - such as the Faithful Companions of Jesus (1839), the Sacred Heart and Notre Dame Sisters (1842 and 1845). There were also new native congregations, including the Sisters of the Infant Jesus, the Dominicans of St Catherine of Siena (1844) and the Society of the Holy Child Jesus, who started in Derby in 1846.

In 1850 there were some 20 different orders of women at work in England and Wales. Between them they had 53 houses. By 1873 there were 235 convents and some 3000 sisters. By 1900 the total had risen to some 600 convents and perhaps 10,000 sisters belonging to 90 orders. By 1950 there were 140 female orders represented in this country and 1075 convents. In 1850 eight women's orders were engaged in teaching. Many of their schools were

small and provided, at most, elementary education. By 1948 there were 336 girls' schools listed in the Association of Convent Schools (with a minimum of 50 pupils) catering for 27,000 Catholic girls, 20,000 non-Catholics and several thousand small boys. Nuns also ran eleven teacher-training colleges with a total population of 1300 students.[1]

Many more foreign orders had meanwhile established themselves in England, including the Ursulines (1851), the Sisters of Charity of St Vincent de Paul (1857), the La Retraite Sisters and the Sisters of the Sacred Hearts of Jesus and Mary, the Ladies of Mary and the Poor Sisters of Nazareth. To these had been added another wave of native orders, including the Sisters of the Cross and Passion, and the Poor Servants of the Mother of God.

✤

The history of female religious in nineteenth- and twentieth-century Britain has yet to be fully told. Much of it has so far been 'invisible', not least because most sisters have been too busy attending to the needs of today and tomorrow to want to dedicate time or resources to recording the past; partly because, to do so might have seemed at odds with the selflessness and anonymity which were goals of those who served the Lord in their consecrated life.

Yet without the often heroic self-sacrifice of thousands of Irish, French and English women who laboured in the Vineyard - often little noticed or thanked, and mostly buried in graves marked by the plainest of crosses - the flowering of the renewed English Catholicism which came to its climax in the post-World War II years would have been impossible. Pope Pius XI is said to have exclaimed, 'We have lost the working classes'. That was less than true in this country than elsewhere thanks especially to that multitude of women who taught and catechised, rescued and nursed the poorest and least privileged in the towns and cities of Victorian and post-Victorian Britain.

The story contains famous names: Catherine McAuley, for instance, who brought the Sisters of Mercy to England: Margaret Hallahan who founded the Dominicans of St Catherine of Siena in Coventry in 1844; Elizabeth Prout, co-founder in Manchester of the Sisters of the Holy Family; Cornelia Connelly, the extraordinary American who founded the Society of the Holy Child. And there is also Geneviève Dupuis, who came to Banbury from France in 1847 with two companions and thereby launched the Congregation of the Sisters of Charity of St Paul the Apostle in this country.

✤

The Sisters of St Paul of Chartres, the congregation to which Geneviève Dupuis belonged, was a typical example of the dozens of new communities dedicated to the active apostolate that had emerged in France during the seventeenth century. It was the result of the response of a devout noble lady, Marie Anne de Tilly, to a plea from her parish priest to provide some elementary education for young girls of the village. To the dismay of those who thought that a woman of high birth should not live and work among peasants, Marie Anne consented. By 1700, a small, informal group of high-minded women had gathered around her. They taught, they did some nursing, and visited the sick; they prayed and studied together. Marie Anne died a mere 38-year-old in 1703, but her school survived, as did the quasi-community which she had drawn together.

In 1708 the then Bishop of Chartres invited the Sisters to his city, provided a house for them and entrusted them to the protection of St Paul. They immediately opened a free elementary school for poor children. By 1727 they had seventeen houses in France and a contingent of sisters had set sail for Guiana to look after a hospital and a school in Cayenne. By the early nineteenth century, having survived the tumults of the French Revolution, the order was establishing itself in the Indian Ocean and Caribbean, and would soon venture to the Far East - with a mission to Hong Kong in 1848. Marie Anne de

The Voice of Geneviève Dupuis

'Do your very best for the children'
- Geneviève Dupuis

Tilly's informal lay community had (long since) developed into a farflung religious order dedicated to teaching, nursing and tending the poor. It was a story which has been repeated many times.

The circumstances of the arrival of the Sisters in England was also a familiar one. They were invited by a zealous parish priest, supported by his bishop, to meet the urgent needs of his flock. Even as the local curé had invoked the help of Marie Anne de Tilly 150 years previously, a Father Tandy of Banbury turned to descendants of Marie Anne in Chartres for aid. Most of the new foundations of nuns in nineteenth-century Britain, whether indigenous communities of Irish or foreign origin were similarly sponsored.

Fr Tandy had only recently been appointed to Banbury. His parish stretched far afield in north Oxfordshire and south-west Warwickshire, an area which had maintained a high level of Catholic allegiance during penal times, so much so that he had seriously considered founding his own community of Sisters to serve the needs of his flock. He had set up a school for poor girls adjoining his church, with a Hannah Young in charge, and also a fee-paying school which a certain Sister Mary Norbert ran. He presumably planned an 'order' to staff the schools and no doubt undertake other works of charity. He eventually decided to look to Chartres

for help.

Mary Norbert seems to have come from Cambridge, where another priest, a Benedictine called Norbert Woolfrey, had been asking for sisters from Chartres since 1843 - without success. Either before or since then, Mary Norbert and her sister had themselves gone to Chartres in the hope of joining the order there. The story is unclear, but it is interesting that the order was well enough known in England for two English women to seek to enter it. Whether they intended to stay in France or to found an English mission is not known.

In the event the two returned home without having been admitted but retaining their names in religion (viz. 'Sister Mary Norbert' and 'Sister Mary Winifred') and still fervent supporters of the order which had refused them. According to Fr Tandy, Sister Mary Norbert strove for some years to establish a branch of the order in England - and it was she who, having somehow come to Banbury and taken on the direction of a school there, seems to have helped to persuade the parish priest to try where Fr Woolfrey had failed.

There was another factor. The auxiliary bishop of the Midlands District, Nicholas Wiseman (soon to be first Archbishop of Westminster) was able to write to Fr Tandy, 'I know the Sisters of

Chartres well. They are just the Sisters for you'. How he made their acquaintance is not told. But his recommendation was no doubt decisive.[2]

By September 1846 Chartres had agreed to send two or three sisters soon. There was an exchange of episcopal correspondence between Birmingham and Chartres confirming the arrangements and a visit from Père Sureau, Superior of the order, to England to finalise details. Two Sisters were chosen: Geneviève Dupuis and Joseph Marie Sapiens. They arrived in Banbury on Saturday 26 June 1847, accompanied by an English woman called Jane Allitt, who was another unsuccessful postulant of the order but now acted as interpreter. The newcomers were accommodated in the presbytery, which had been enlarged and refurbished to house them. Fr Tandy had moved out to the home of a parishioner.

Two, not three, Sisters had come from Chartres. It seems clear that Sister Mary Norbert expected that she would join them and thus achieve a long-standing ambition. The same seems to have been true of the other hitherto disappointed candidate, Jane Allitt. Moreover - and astonishingly - three weeks or so before the Chartres Sisters arrived, Hannah Young had been admitted to the order. Presumably Sister

taken it upon herself to allow her to enter.

Hannah Young persevered and had a long and fruitful apostolate, dying in 1906 aged 83. As for the other two, both were finally turned away by Fr Tandy. Jane Allitt was clearly unsuitable. The other, wrote Père Sureau, 'has no vocation'. She was not to be professed, even though she had a warm affection for Mother Dupuis.[3]

Thus began the mission to Banbury: two young nuns arrived from France with little English and a daunting range of tasks ahead - and to form a small community beset by complex human tensions and emotions. But what had been begun was to grow into one of the most remarkable enterprises undertaken by any order of sisters in any land.

The Mustard Seed

A mustard seed had been sown. Within six years there were eight branch houses. By 1864 there were 26 and the Congregation numbered 116. By 1890 there were 52 houses and 384 Sisters spread over almost all the dioceses of England and Wales. This fast expansion was achieved despite inevitable false starts and disappointments. The first offshoot - in Brighton - failed within two years. The second, in Leamington Spa, nearly foundered on the insistence of the patron, a Mrs Bishop, on exercising more control than Mother Geneviève would accept. In the end she yielded and the Sisters opened a school which they ran for 132 years. In 1853 their first school was launched in Birmingham, which lasted for 129 years, and in 1854 a school in Radford which closed after 108 years. 1859 was something of an annus mirabilis, with seven new foundations, including those in Southport and Holywell, which achieved 138 years each, and Bradford (130 years). But of the 88 houses founded by Mother Geneviève, no less than 37 were closed by her for one reason or another - including what were regarded as excessive interference or demands by clergy. 52 were functioning at her death in 1903 and 14 have survived to 1997.

The Sisters came to Banbury to teach. They took over a free school for the poor and a private, i.e. fee-paying, one. The second generated funds to sustain the first. Later they would move into secondary education and teacher-training. Moreover they soon embarked upon what was to become a major part of their apostolate, the care of orphans. The story began in the village of Radford, Oxfordshire, where two Sisters who had gone to run a parish school there took into their care a few destitute children. Soon this had developed into an orphanage for 35 children, thanks not least to a chance legacy from a local priest.

In 1876 the Sisters opened a second orphanage in Avon Dassett, Warwickshire, which the generosity of a local Catholic couple and a loan made possible. Eight years later, Bishop Ullathorne committed to their care his first so-called Poor Law School, St Paul's at Coleshill, for abandoned children. All this paved the way for the establishment of the Birmingham Rescue Society, later known as Father Hudson's Homes, in which the Sisters played a priceless part. What Father Hudson, its chief inspiration, himself described as a 'garden city' for children, with farms, hospitals, schools, boys' and girls' homes, would eventually be established; and for decades on average over sixty Sisters worked there, teaching and nursing.

The Sisters never forgot their initial concern: to provide elementary education for the Catholic poor - the 'three Rs', housecraft, needlework and, above all, learning the Catechism in parish schools all over the country. Over the years many tens of thousands of children were to receive free primary education at their knees.

Devoted to the young, Mother Geneviève quickly realised after arriving in Banbury that the many poor girls who were forced to go out to work would not be served by day schools, and so took the novel step of providing evening classes also. Eventually the larger schools extended their age-range and began to admit young boys as well, though the Foundress, strongly supported by the bishop of Birmingham, refused to take on schools exclusively for boys.

The schools were essentially parish schools. Two or three Sisters would be sent - usually at the invitation of a parish priest - to open what were often, at least to begin with, humble ventures. They were the only institute in England, Bishop Ullathorne noted, in which 'so small a number are placed together [to work] in poorer missions which could not sustain a convent.' Inevitably some of the establishments grew large and communities of ten or more became not uncommon. But the order never lost its commitment to sending out Sisters in twos or threes to often the poorest parishes, to teach the young to read and write, and instruct them in the Faith, often in very modest buildings, and often at the cost of much hardship to themselves. They were, often enough, the heroic pioneers, trail-blazers. No less strikingly, they were never merely school-teachers. In the evenings and on Saturdays they regularly visited the sick and housebound, instructed adults, distributed food and clothing which they had collected for the poor - their pupils and families, and parishioners generally.

Below: Earliest group photograph at Selly Park in the archives. Date unknown.

Above: Selly Park. Earliest photograph showing original mansion with the first part of the cloister as far as the front door, clock, built in 1880s. (The foundation stone may be seen on the right side of the front door. With the cloister is the large refectory. Upstairs was the large novitiate room, now St. Peter's; the chapel, now Our Lady Immaculate; the corridor outside the chapel, now Our Lady's Landing; St. Geneviève's Cloister, now the solarium. The door between St. Peter's and Our Lady Immaculate is where the Tabernacle was. Above the chapel was a balcony looking down onto the Sanctuary. This is the present Sacred Heart Dormitory A door and stairs from St. Brigid's led to it, as today.)

They were 'parish sisters' long before that term came into use.

The poor schools were not theirs, but belonged to the parishes; and they themselves usually lived in humble houses among the poor. The order has produced no grand convents, except for its mother house at Selly Park. And that building has been crucial in guaranteeing another distinctive feature of the Congregation, namely, its strong sense of identity and *esprit de corps*. All postulants entered the order at Selly Park, drawn thither from many parts of Britain and Ireland. All served their noviceship, were clothed and professed there, and thence sent to their various posts in branch houses, many returning frequently for various purposes. All had lived there under the same roof as the superior general, knew her and were personally known by her. Many superiors general of other orders resided in remote generalates perhaps as far away as Paris or Rome. Mother Dupuis and her successors have always lived among the large community at Selly Park. They could regularly be seen praying with them in the chapel. They ate with them. They could be button-

holed in the corridor. Moreover Sisters had had a better chance to know one another and to follow the fortunes of Sisters in far-flung places than would have been possible in a less centralised community. Every Sister could hope to return to Selly Park when her earthly pilgrimage neared its end; many, indeed, returned home to die in the mother house where, perhaps decades before, they had first dedicated themselves to the consecrated life.

Two other facts nourished the order's unity. First, most unusually, it had resisted the idea of setting up provinces which, with provincial structures and even novitiates, would inevitably have 'federalised' the order and tended to

distance the superior general from her sisters. Mother Geneviève, as long as her health permitted, like her successors, was in close control of all the order's affairs, visited houses, maintained an extensive and often deeply affectionate correspondence with her daughters, especially the local superiors of branch houses. All this also meant that major decisions could be made and executed more swiftly than was possible in orders which had more elaborate structures. Secondly, unlike many French orders, Chartres had known no distinction between 'choir nuns' and lowlier 'soeurs' and so the English Sisters of St Paul also grew up without what could sometimes be a painful division within the community based on social as well as educational criteria. The Sisters of St Paul, though mindful of the variety of gifts of the Spirit, guarded the oneness of the body. Postulants were expected to bring dowries with them. These, plus contributions from branch houses, were Selly Park's major source of necessary income. But many arrived with little cash and only a handful of personal possessions. None was ever refused because her family was too poor to endow her.

Separate on Earth United in Heaven

Strictly speaking, none of the new orders produced by the Catholic Reformation (and since) was an 'order' in the full canonical sense. Moreover, the post-Reformation female orders had had a stormy time trying to secure acceptance by the ecclesiastical Establishment of their vision of their apostolate. The foundress of the Ursulines, like Mary Ward, had initially envisaged a formation much closer to today's Secular Institutes than medieval nunneries. She wanted no distinctive dress, no solemn vows and, most importantly, no enclosure.

In the end, after much heart-searching and suffering, a compromise emerged. The new orders acquired some structures and habits, but only simple vows and often minimal claustral restriction. Some, like the Sisters of Mercy, remained simply a collection of autonomous houses. Some quickly became centralised international bodies. Most were diocesan congregations under the jurisdiction of the local bishop.

It is clear that the Chartres Sisters fell into this last category. They saw themselves as primarily servants of their diocese. Though the bishop was their 'general' in practice the order was

Left: The Cloister as it looked before refurbishment with grey and white flagstones, red brick walls and heating vents.

"My Dear Reverend Mother..."

'My own ideal ... is to have a Novitiate House in every important diocese.'
- William Ullathorne, 8 July 1864

directed by his nominee, known as the Father Superior, who was a priest. These Superiors had shaped the order's evolution. They controlled admission and appointments of sisters, and had oversight of all the order's affairs. Thus when Fr Tandy turned to them for help, he wrote to the Superior, Père Sureau, and it was he who handled all the negotiations. He wrote to Dr Tandy of 'our Sisters' and said, 'I am quite willing to give you some'. And it was he who told Mother Dupuis from a distance, and in no uncertain terms, to be rid of Jane Allitt and Sister Mary Norbert.[4]

The mother house in Chartres had, of course, set up branch houses. They were mostly - to begin with - inside the diocese. Foundations further afield in practice were (or became) independent and subject to their local bishop. This had first happened when a house opened near Strasbourg and what proved to be a vigorous, separate community was established.

In 1846 Père Sureau had clearly indicated that the despatch of sisters from Chartres to Banbury would lead to an independent English Congregation. 'I am quite willing', he wrote to Dr Tandy, 'to give you some of our sisters to begin a Congregation like ours'. But how far everyone else appreciated that this would be the first step to founding an independent community is another matter, not least because the English

venture would obviously require much spiritual and material support - support that was gladly given - for years. The first English postulants received their formation in Chartres, the latter sent more of its own Sisters to England, and when the apparently Heaven-sent opportunity arose in 1849 to acquire a very suitable building as a residence, namely, St John's Priory - and to move out of Dr Tandy's presbytery into their own home nearby - Chartres generously lent the necessary £1700.

Mother Dupuis never lost her deep affection for her own mother house and visited it as often as she could. For years after her arrival in England she sought and received spiritual direction from it. When France was threatened with major political upset in 1870-1 she offered refuge in England to the community from which she had sprung. Final canonical separation of the English Congregation, as we shall see, had come in 1864. One who had been 'a very dear daughter' was now 'dear mother' of her own children and her community a beloved sister of the French one, who was 'your senior Sister'. The Superior General in Chartres, writing of the 'dear Community of which you are the mother,' could add, perhaps wistfully, that she prayed that the 'two families of St Paul, though distinct on earth, might be united in Heaven'. Another General would write in 1888, twenty-five years later, 'the English Community is very dear to me ... I present it to the good God and to Our Blessed Lady with the French one. I cannot separate them in my heart.' For her part, Geneviève Dupuis followed the fortunes of the French houses closely, and continued to receive newsletters from Chartres. In 1872 she asked Chartres for another huge loan with which to set up an orphanage - a project realised at Avon Dassett (Warks) - and as late as 1895 was thanking the French Father Superior for 'instructions on the renewal of vows'.[5]

Years before, in 1848, the Mother General of Chartres had given her approval to the use of a 'cap and cloak' for outdoor wear, to make the Sisters' religious dress, still unlawful in Protestant England, 'invisible', but had pleaded that the habit given by 'our founder' should be used indoors. She even added that she would prefer not to have foundations in England if this resulted in 'a serious breach of time-honoured usage.' However, Père Sureau had bidden her to add that this was not a command but only 'an observation for you to consider,' and she herself had already conceded that Sister Geneviève's infant community, before itself becoming a mother house, should adopt the dress which seemed suitable to its founder, i.e. Dr Tandy - as it did. Dr Tandy had insisted that the French habit was ill-suited to England. Bishop Ullathorne later explained why, in a characteristically vigorous way : 'it was like that of the women enclosed in prisons and workhouses in England and, had it been continued, it would have brought such contempt upon them by the great mass of Protestants that they would not have been able to appear in the streets or in the schools.'[6]

Bishop Ullathorne, from the start, had clearly regarded the community at Banbury and its growing number of branch houses as directly under his jurisdiction. Dr Tandy had expressed this succinctly. 'The order established here [in Banbury] is dependant [sic] entirely upon you', he had written to Bishop Ullathorne in November 1848. The Sisters 'will have their mother house in England whenever your Lordship thinks proper to establish it, and you will be the head of the order in England.'[7] Though the authorities in Chartres, especially Père Sureau, accepted that the English community would be independent - eventually - they may well have envisaged that complete autonomy would be achieved only when it was fully 'indigenised', as we would say today, and no French Sisters were working for it any longer. Indeed,

Bishop Ullathorne

there is evidence that, ten years after the Banbury mission was launched, Chartres was preparing to recall Mother Geneviève and the two French Sisters still with her. Only this fully explains the urgent tone of a letter from Ullathorne to the bishop of Chartres imploring the latter to allow these three, who were at that moment in Chartres (had they actually been recalled to their mother house?) to 'remain in England ... and, as a crowning favour ... definitively and permanently make over the Superioress and the two French Sisters now with her, with their consent, to the English branch of the Institute ... which will ever retain a filial affection and sense of duty to the French Institute'. Ullathorne's plea was granted.[8]

The independence of the English Congregation, formally conceded by Rome in 1864, was ratified by the establishment of its mother house in Selly Park in the same year. As early as 1849 Ullathorne had indicated to Mother Geneviève that a 'head house in Birmingham' was 'precisely what I want', but instead, the Sisters had acquired a property in Banbury and nothing more is heard of a move to the bishop's city for over 12 years. When the property at Selly Park was first mentioned, Bishop Ullathorne had asked whether it was not too far from Birmingham and later proposed buying land and buildings in Perry Bar. On 14 February 1864 he was enthusiastic for Selly Park and had

'changed all my opinion about taking ground at Perry Bar', because the price of land there had soared. He had decided 'that £5000 should be offered for it at once.' Six weeks later he had decided that the Sisters should purchase the house with eight acres instead of the original $16^3/4$, whereupon the vendor apparently raised the price to £5500. 'I do not like the bargain at all, or the house or place', Bishop Ullathorne suddenly declared on 9 July 1864, and instead proposed to sell the Sisters four or five acres of diocesan land in Aston, near Perry Bar even though he had assured Mother Geneviève in May 1864, shortly after she returned home from her heroic visit to Rome, that Selly Hall had been secured.[9]

But Mother Geneviève had her way. The deal was eventually concluded and the Sisters acquired a new mother house. Preaching at the opening of Selly Park, Ullathorne recalled: 'Many things conspired against the transition of your mother house to this locality; but your Superiors [that is, Mother Geneviève and Dr Tandy] prayed at the tombs of the Holy Apostles, Saints Peter and Paul, [during their recent stay in Rome] for its accomplishment, and thus the house was purchased at a time when everything was contrary to it.' Whether his own role in this story had been unfailingly helpful is another matter.[10]

Rome Must Speak: Trials and Tribulations

The fast expansion of the Congregation inevitably raised an important canonical question. Granted that the Sisters of St Paul were neither establishing a network of effectively autonomous houses as were the Sisters of Mercy, nor dividing into provinces, as did many other orders, what was to be the relationship with the bishop of Birmingham of the growing number of branch houses which lay outside his diocese? As has been said, Bishop Ullathorne was clearly persuaded that Mother Geneviève and her Sisters were subject to his jurisdiction and exercised the same oversight over admissions, clothings and professions, and the rest of the order's affairs as did the bishop of Chartres over the French community. Like him, he expected to give and be asked for advice and consent on every aspect of the Congregation's life. And just as the bishop of Chartres exercised his control through the Father Superior, a senior priest of the diocese, so Bishop Ullathorne delegated much day-to-day guidance of the Sisters to Mother Dupuis' friend and confidant, and in truth co-founder of the English mission, Dr William Tandy.

All this made sense as long as the Sisters of Chartres, who, like Geneviève Dupuis herself, had promised to serve in that diocese, had indeed done so, or the Sisters of the English Congregation worked only within the diocese of Birmingham. What happened when the latter moved into other dioceses? Ullathorne believed that, though the local bishops would be consulted, the Sisters would remain subjects of Selly Park over which he had full oversight, and were only temporarily answerable to local ordinaries. In his view, the order's Father Superior, his nominee, oversaw the whole Congregation on his behalf and the bishop of Birmingham as ordinary had the right to provide over its General Chapters.

Ullathorne was not so much jealous of his own authority as concerned to protect the unity of the new Congregation. But if the Sisters, wherever they were, remained ultimately subject of the bishop of Birmingham, local bishops were faced with a new form of that dilution of their authority within their own dioceses which had vexed relations between religious orders and bishops down the centuries, except that, on this occasion, the ordinaries' complaints would be directed at a fellow-bishop rather than the religious concerned. The latter would be caught in cross-fire.

Crucial to Ullathorne's case was the claim that the Congregation's branch houses in other dioceses consisted of only two or three Sisters teaching in

Geneviève Dupuis in her younger days

parish schools rather than their own large institutions, and were best described as 'missions'. The Sisters expected to return to Selly Park to end their days there and perhaps he also meant that they might expect to hand over to others once their pioneering work was done. The difficulty with this argument was that some of the branch houses already had eight, ten or more Sisters - and the totals could be expected to grow as schools flourished - and that the Congregation was striking deep roots in an increasing number of distant places. Moreover, Bishop Ullathorne's case did not persuade Rome

❧

In 1860 the Bishop of Chartres petitioned the Holy See, that is, the Congregation for Bishops and Regulars, for approval of his order. Why he had not done so before and why he did so then is not known. Nor is it clear how he saw his role in the daily life of a Congregation which had numerous foundations in Western Europe, many of them daughters of Chartres' daughter in Strasbourg. In the event, Rome granted general approval of the aims and work of the order (what was called a brief 'laudatif') in 1861, but withheld final approbation of its Rules and Constitution - this for a number of reasons, including the fact that the Sisters did not take perpetual vows and that they retained the right to dispose of possessions by will or otherwise.

When Mother Geneviève heard of the bishop of Chartres' initiative she evidently saw this as an opportunity - or perhaps something more urgent? - for her to secure Roman recognition of her community and wrote to the bishop of Chartres asking that the English Rule be submitted along with the French, which it followed closely. Predictably, the reply was that the right person to act on her behalf was the bishop of Birmingham. Why Mother Geneviève had not invoked his help from the start is unclear. Yet more remarkably, she had evidently broached the idea to the bishop of Chartres that she might go to Rome in person to seek papal approval. That produced firm episcopal discouragement. The bishop also warned that the Holy See would grant only a brief laudatif initially. 'Many communities go no further', he said, adding prophetically that full approval of a Rule required 'judicial investigation and long and difficult formalities.'[11]

Since Bishop Ullathorne happened to be in Rome on other business in late 1861, Mother Geneviève decided to turn to him for help and, undeterred by the warning from Chartres, to seek full papal approval of the Congregation and its Rule. This, Ullathorne knew, would have to be sought via the Congregation for the Propagation of the Faith ('Propaganda'), which was still responsible for English affairs, not the Congregation for Bishops and Regulars, to which the bishop of Chartres had had recourse.

✢

In reply, Ullathorne spoke frankly about the problems which he foresaw, namely, that of reconciling 'the exigencies of the other dioceses' where branch houses existed with 'the principle of one Central House to which all belong', and of providing that 'monies left expressly for those localities are not removable, although those left to the Sisters themselves may go towards the maintenance of the parent house in the event of the Sisters being removed.' He added: 'there is considerable jealousy in Rome as well as elsewhere about the interference with the rights of ordinaries over nuns.' Nothing short of giving bishops 'the full recognition of the rights of visitation will content them.' As for what 'Sisters can and what they cannot take away' in the event of withdrawing from a branch house, 'perhaps I had better not touch it.' He would nonetheless petition for approval of the order as 'the English Congregation of Sisters of St Paul' and Mother Geneviève's 'superiority for life as foundress.'

Three days later, on 12 December 1861, he was sending a different message. The Rule which she had sent him - so he now discovered - was essentially the French one and took no account of English practice. It presumed that the Sisters worked in only one

diocese and did not provide for perpetual vows. If presented to the Roman authorities it would surely fail. The entire text ' must undergo a sifting', he concluded rather brusquely. 'Nothing else will do'. On his return he would come to Banbury to discuss the matter.[12]

Bishop Ullathorne was clearly envisaging a thorough re-drafting of the French Rule. Shortly afterwards, however, he had a discussion with the prefect of Propaganda, Cardinal Barnabò, which caused him to propose a new way in which 'to accomplish our plan'. Writing to Mother Dupuis from the English College on 7 January 1862, he proposed that a petition for approval of the Congregation, apart from the Rule, should be accompanied by a 'brief statement' of the 'differences of observance' from the French Congregation. 'We shall then get a recognition as a distinct body and on distinct grounds', separate 'from France', and thus allow for the Rule to be matured at leisure and its confirmation obtained later, he explained. Three weeks later (28 January 1862) Ullathorne despatched the petition from Mother Dupuis to the Congregation for Bishops and Regulars via Propaganda with a covering letter that praised her and her Sisters warmly and listed the changes which had been made to the French Rule to suit English conditions.

These included adopting a habit of

Father William Tandy

black serge and a white guimpe, the introduction of perpetual simple vows and a noviceship of one year in the mother house, and such minor changes as deletion of the rule that Sisters should eat whatever was placed before them even if it was 'repugnant'. Ullathorne underlined, once again, that the branch houses should be viewed as missions, 'pioneers in those places where regular convents with complete communities and with novitiates are not established'. Later he would say that the Sisters had 'but one home' and other residences were but 'temporary abodes'. Though dependants of the mother house, branch houses were to be visited by local ordinaries and subject to them 'in all that concerns the branch establishments', and all local endowments would be 'left behind in the event of the Sisters withdrawing'. Nonetheless the bishop of Birmingham had the right to authorise, and once or twice had authorised, 'the superioress to recall the Sisters from an establishment to the mother house.'[13]

❧

Roman wheels turn slowly. After perusal by Propaganda, Bishop Ullathorne's petition was sent on to Bishops and Regulars for a decision. There it got 'stuck' for twelve months. Eventually, on 5 March 1863, Cardinal Barnabò wrote to Ullathorne that Bishops and Regulars had at last responded with fourteen 'Animadversions',

which set out serious reservations about his submission of January 1862. By July 1863 the bishop had framed his response to them. Once again he reiterated his claim that all the Sisters of the Congregation 'belonged' to a single mother house and were posted in other dioceses only 'temporarily and almost as in missions'. He had refined his explanation of his own role within the order thus: as bishop of Birmingham he had direct jurisdiction over the 'central house' but indirect jurisdiction over Sisters in houses in other dioceses. He ended a long letter with this astonishing suggestion - the Superior General, Mother Dupuis, should herself come to Rome to receive the approbation of her Congregation. She would 'present herself to Your Eminence in the month of November', accompanied by Dr Tandy.

Would that we knew the whole story behind this brief announcement. It is difficult to suppose that the idea of the foundress going to Rome herself originated with the bishop, though later Mother Geneviève would say that she was acting on his 'orders'. Since she had made the proposal quite independently to the bishop of Chartres two and a half years previously, is it not likely that, exasperated by the delays and toings and froings, she now revived her idea and persuaded the bishop to give his consent? It is worth pausing to reflect on what she was proposing. She, a

---

"My Dear Reverend Mother..."

"God is shaping your order in your lifetime, so that no unhallowed hand may mishandle it afterwards.'
- Fr Samuel Sole, Chipping Norton, 13 February 1898

humble superior of what was still a minor order in a fairly remote corner of the world (in Rome's estimation), would make her way to Rome, accompanied by a mere parish priest, would storm her way past curial bureaucrats to a cardinal-prefect of a Sacred Congregation and ask for papal confirmation, not just 'laudation', of her Institute, its Rule and Constitutions. That is what she sought : not a brief laudatif, but full approval of the revised English Rule - which she had finally translated into French (since Roman officialdom had not yet come to recognise English as an important language) after her arrival in the Eternal City. Ignatius Loyola had gone to Rome in person to seek endorsement of his newly-formed Company of Jesus over three hundred years previously. Some decades later Mary Ward had been incarcerated in Rome because of her vision of the role of female religious in the Church was so novel. Had any founder, let alone foundress, dared to take on the Curia single-handedly, in person, since? Moreover at some point Mother Geneviève conceived the idea of going beyond a mere cardinal. She would, and did, have an audience of the pope himself.

✤

Mother Geneviève, a companion Sister and Dr Tandy arrived in Rome, after a lengthy journey, in November 1863, as Bishop Ullathorne had promised. Dr Tandy had studied in Rome years before and presumably still had some Italian; Mother Geneviève, who had travelled only between Chartres and Banbury in her life, had French and broken English, and was quickly savaged by mosquitoes. Yet the near-miracle happened. The three were received by the official of Propaganda. On 22 November 1864 the unlikely trio had an audience of Pope Pius IX himself. How this was achieved we do not know.

Geneviève's report to the Sisters of this meeting emphasises the graciousness of a holy pope and her reverence towards him. But Dr Tandy, in a private account, recalled that the indomitable Frenchwoman may have been awed but not over-awed. Rather, she stuck to the reason for this historic encounter, namely, that His Holiness should give his blessing to her enterprise. So, when the pope, after the initial formalities, said that the matter should go to the Congregation for the Bishops and Regulars, she boldly replied that, no, it should go to Propaganda, for this was the Congregation which handled English affairs. Whereupon the pope replied, no, it was a matter for Bishops and Regulars. And that was that. Not many people of either sex, lay or clerical, have stood their ground thus before a pope.[14]

The courage which had inspired her pilgrimage to Rome was to be tested yet further in the months that followed the papal audience.

Pope Pius IX

Rome Has Spoken: Trials Anew

Having negotiated the setting up of a structured Church in Australia in his thirties and then been charged by his brother-bishops with securing the restoration of the English hierarchy in 1850, Bishop Ullathorne was probably as well versed in the ways of the Curia as any outsider. He had guessed that, behind any particular difficulties in Canon Law concerning relations between Selly Park and branch houses, or the bishop of Birmingham and other ordinaries, there loomed a larger and more general one, namely, Rome's anxiety about the proliferation of new religious institutes in recent decades and the conviction that this had to be curbed. So when he had spoken of the English Congregation of Sisters of Charity as 'similar to that of Chartres' but 'entirely independent of the French superiors', he had known he had to face the challenge of showing why yet another new foundation was justified.

In a letter to Dr Tandy he had indicated that Roman reluctance, as a matter of principle, to approve new orders was only part of the problem, however. Perhaps, he mused, letters had been written from France (i.e. Chartres itself) 'against your being independent of them.' There is no evidence that this had happened and we may never know

why the bishop suspected it. But if there had been a last-minute and, humanly speaking, understandable reluctance on the part of the mother finally to be parted from her daughter there was a second reason for proceeding circumspectly. One thing had been clear: the objective was 'laudation' not complete approbation. And since English affairs were handled by Propaganda it was necessary to proceed via that Congregation. But since Propaganda was especially resistant to the multiplication of new orders, the supplication for papal approval should be addressed to Bishops and Regulars, though it would have to reach there via Propaganda. Since the French institute had already received approval by Bishops and Regulars, the English would stand a good chance of receiving its blessing, too.[15]

That had been Ullathorne's final plan of action. Shortly afterwards Mother Geneviève had boldly decided to break the impasse and go to Rome herself. But now that the pope had ruled that Bishops and Regulars had sole cognisance of the matter Ullathorne could no longer be actively involved. 'It is an essential point of our policy to communicate only with Propaganda', he explained. So Dr Tandy would have to take charge. He should deliver the following argument to Bishops and Regulars, Ullathorne urged: the English Congregation was established and had existed as a distinct and independent body for fourteen years before the French Institute was approved by the Holy See; when that happened the English community was not treated as part of it and, except for the foundress, all the French had returned to France; hence the order consisted now 'exclusively of English subjects.' No claim had ever been made by Chartres to authority over the English institute, Ullathorne wanted Tandy to stress, nor would the bishop of Birmingham have admitted any such claim.

Was Ullathorne fearful that the Congregation for Bishops and Regulars would refuse approval of a separate English community altogether, i.e. that the survival of the Sisters of Charity in England as a separate entity was at stake? It seems likely. But there is no doubt about his exasperation at the treatment which had been meted out. In a remarkably frank outcry, perhaps born of his many years of dealing with Roman officialdom, he added : 'I attach no importance to the snubbing treatment, nor ought you, for its object is to get at the spirit of the Reverend Mother. It is a common Roman trick and will be changed after a while to a kinder tone ... patience and perseverenance [sic] are the stock-in-trade of all who deal with Rome. Take all good-naturedly ... much depends on this spirit of confidence with which you stick to your point.'

Neither Mother Geneviève nor Dr Tandy was easily beaten. Despite what the pope himself had directed, they went back to Propaganda and asked its president, Cardinal Barnabò to make a second attempt to persuade the pope to allow the matter to be settled by his Congregation, which he did. The pope again refused; whereupon Barnabò told them they had no choice but to submit to Bishops and Regulars.

Their first encounter with this other Congregation was not a happy one. Its secretary, so Dr Tandy reported, 'rated us soundly' for wanting to be separated from France. So, fears that Bishop Ullathorne may have had that the very survival of an independent English Community was at risk, were well founded. However, because the official had little French (and presumably no English), it was impossible to progress far with the discussion. A second meeting went much more satisfactorily. Accompanied by a good Italian-speaker, the rector of the Irish College, the delegation from England encountered another, but sympathetic, secretary who suggested that, if Propaganda were to certify that there were no essential differences between the French and English Rules, .then, since Bishops and Regulars had approved the former, there should be no obstacle in the way of approving the latter. Dr Tandy, however, countered by asking that, instead of being passed back to

"*My Dear Reverend Mother...*"

'*You must not hasten the day of trouble but keep your heart in patience. Distress not yourself with vague apprehensions of wrong ... resign yourself with patience. Let not your fears haunt you, but dismiss them.*'
- *William Ullathorne,*
26 June 1863

Propaganda, the matter could be settled by a 'consultor', that is, an individual expert. This was agreed. The consultor acted quickly. By 29 January 1864 the recommendation by the Bishops and Regulars that the English Sisters of Charity be granted papal approval had been accepted by the pope and the papal fiat notified back to the Roman Congregation.[16]

This had now to be translated into a papal brief. Mother Geneviève had been writing home 'Oh! what a slow business is ours ... Oh! patience! we want patience,' and later 'God tries us just a little now. May he be praised forever. It is just that I should have to suffer for my sins and for those of my children. Pray for us. Do not fear. All will end well, but we must practise patience.' 'My dear Child' she wrote on 13 February 1864, 'we want patience in the Holy City. We thought our affairs nearly finished, and lo! we have no idea when they will be at an end'.

In truth, since her arrival in Rome three months previously, a great deal had been accomplished - by Roman standards if not hers - and though the further delay tried her sorely, she had to wait only until 5 March for the papal brief to be produced. Seven days later she could write joyfully : 'now we belong to the Church by a special adoption. We are approved by the Holy See.'[17]

She and Dr Tandy returned home with an understandable sense of achievement. They had made history. She had done what probably no other foundress had dared to do. But the papal brief was 'laudatif' only. Exactly as the bishop of Chartres had predicted several years before, Rome had given its blessing to the overall work of the English Congregation of Sisters of Charity and implicitly ratified its independence from Chartres, but had not given final approval to the Rule. That, as the brief explained, was deferred to 'a more opportune time'. Moreover, when the brief was handed to Dr Tandy (not Mother Geneviève) it was accompanied by a sealed letter to the bishop of Birmingham containing nineteen 'Observations' on that Rule. Effectively, these were amendments which would be required before final approbation could be granted.

Some were minor or procedural - that debts incurred by the Sisters be approved by the Holy See and dispensations from vows reserved to it, for example. Some touched the daily lives of the Sisters. Among these was a strange ruling that they should use 'some pious book' or life of a saint for spiritual reading rather than Sacred Scripture, another that they should not seek permission to receive Holy Communion or go to Confession on their knees, others that the office of the dead should be recited on Thursdays, not Sundays, and that vows should initially be made for three years and then life.

Other changes would have a major impact on the part played by the bishop of Birmingham in the life of the Congregation. In the first place, though he retained his right to preside over General Chapters, he would do so as 'a delegate of the Holy See' and not by virtue of his ordinary jurisdiction. The term 'delegate of the Holy See' had been prominent in decrees of the Council of Trent which, while guaranteeing or restoring bishops' authority in their dioceses, bound them more closely to Rome and made them more dependent on the Apostolic See. Ullathorne perceived that, if he henceforth could preside over General Chapters and elections only by virtue of delegated powers, he and his successors could not aid or advise the superior general, as of right, in any matter that concerned 'the Congregation generally.' This interpretation was confirmed by the further rulings that the right of election of the superior general was vested solely in the General Chapter, that the latter was to chose four Assistants who constituted the Council, and that the mistress of novices was to be chosen by the Council and appointed by the superior general. Most importantly of all, perhaps, there would henceforth be no father superior nominated by the bishop of Birmingham to exercise immediate oversight of the order on

behalf of the ordinary. Rome had set its face against all such appointments. Thus it had not only ratified the English Congregation's independence from Chartres. It had made the Congregation largely independent of the bishop of Birmingham. Henceforth, Ullathorne concluded, the latter would be unable to 'direct, aid or advise her [the superior general] himself or authorise anyone else to do so. She stands alone in whatever concerns the general government [of the order]'.

Every bishop would be 'the superior of the house within the limits of his diocese.' Bishop Ullathorne had conceded that long before and had acknowledged that all ordinaries, himself included, would have the right of visitation of convents situated in their dioceses; but he had not expected that his own special role in overseeing and directing the affairs of the order would be so drastically reduced, particularly by 'the prohibition to nominate any father superior.'[18]

It is important to appreciate why he felt dismay at this ruling. By it, he explained, 'a woman is left to stand alone with all the responsibilities of her Congregation upon her and with no Ecclesiastical Authority or advice to have recourse to on this side of Rome', and no priest to act as 'prudent medium' between the Congregation and clergy who, 'so often, from ignorance of what

The Voice of Geneviève Dupuis

'I am desirous that you should become more interior'
- Geneviève Dupuis

"My Dear Reverend Mother..."

'Keep up your heart. Your trials
will fatten your soul.'
- William Ullathorne in Rome,
21 December 1862

religious life requires, cause affliction and distress to the Sisters and imperil the establishments. He was not lamenting reduction of his own authority so much as pointing out the vulnerability of the newly-enfranchised order when the protection afforded by him and the father superior was removed. Nor was he implying that the female religious were 'second-class.' Rather, he was frankly and shrewdly pointing to the need for his and a priest's protection in the ecclesiastical world in which they lived. He was putting their welfare first.

✤

The story of the Sisters' quest for final approval by Rome was to run for almost another 70 years and to take several more twists and turns.

In April 1888, Edward Ilsley, Bishop Ullathorne's recently-appointed auxiliary, indicated that he would like to see Rules and Constitutions of the order given Rome's final approbation at last - during Mother Geneviève's dwindling lifetime - and thus, after 24 years' unexplained interval, set the wheels turning again. As it proved, however, his arrival on the scene and his no doubt well-meaning initiative were to bring new tribulations to Mother Geneviève and her companions.

Only in 1895 was her petition finally presented to the Congregation of Bishops and Regulars, to whom, at the request of Mother Geneviève, all twelve bishops in whose dioceses the 53 houses of the order were located, led by the Cardinal Archbishop of Westminster, sent letters of support. It took nearly three years for Rome to respond. On 1 February 1898 a papal decree of approbation was issued and despatched to Bishop Ilsley.[19]

Mother Dupuis declared at once that the decree 'far exceeded her expectations', but her delight was premature. It did indeed confirm her institute as 'a Congregation of simple vows under the rule of a Mother General' and spoke most appreciatively of its work. But essentially this was simply another commendation 'laudatif'. Once again final approval of the Rule was postponed 'to a more opportune time' and once again there were 'several Animadversions' concerning the Rule which Rome wanted to be taken on board. Several were concerned with minor matters. One required that Sisters be allowed to send sealed letters to the Holy See, the ordinary, the superior general. Another proposed a major innovation, namely, that the order would accept the principle of dividing into provinces. This was to be voted on at the next General Chapter and, if accepted, would result in General Chapters thereafter being composed of provincial superiors and two elected representatives of every province, instead of superiors of branch houses.[20]

Where this idea came from is unknown. Was it from Dr Ilsley?

Fr Samuel Sole of Chipping Norton, Mother Geneviève's closest advisor after the death of Dr Tandy in 1886, was correct when he described the papal decree as a disappointment. But he urged her to yield to Rome's directives and predicted that the final approval was only six months away - optimism indeed.

✤

For reasons which we may never uncover fully, relations between Mother Geneviève and Bishop Ilsley were never good. Possibly the root of the problem was simply incompatibility of personality. Mother Geneviève was warm, spontaneous and volatile; the bishop outwardly cold, cerebral and an addict to canonical detail. Both were devout servants of the Lord in their different ways.

Perhaps something more than a personality clash began in 1888 when the Order's first General Chapter was held. Despite the fact that Rome's 'Observations' of 1864 had provided for meetings of a General Chapter, as long since practised in Chartres, none had taken place. The nearest that the Congregation had got to one was a gathering in 1879 of Superiors of branch houses at which Ullathorne had intended that an Assistant to Mother Geneviève should be chosen (but

formally nominated by him) with a virtual right of succession. However, the bishop suddenly announced that he thought the local Superiors were 'too young and inexperienced to be allowed to vote for the election' and so named no one. One wonders whether this was the whole truth.[21]

Nine years later the first General Chapter was solemnly convened. Was this evidence of a new episcopal broom, Ilsley's, at work? The Chapter appointed four Assistants who would form the Council and have responsibility, with the Superior General, for the administration of the order. General Chapters were to be held every three years. So the Congregation now had an established governance. At the General Chapter of 1894, however, there was a new item on the agenda, namely, the election of the Superior General. Mother Geneviève was re-appointed - but again one wonders why her election was now deemed necessary and whether the hand of a bishop who was always concerned with due process had been at work. Perhaps to secure her position, by the time of the next General Chapter in 1897, Mother Dupuis had secured a ruling from the prefect of Bishops and Regulars that the rule of triennial election did not apply to her as foundress of the order. The cardinal was obviously responding to a request from her and in turn she was asked to 'show this letter to the bishop to whom I am writing today'. That was on 12 June 1897. In fact that letter to Bishop Ilsley was not sent until 2 August and had an important addition. Mother Geneviève was to hold office for life 'subject to the approval of the ordinary', i.e. the bishop of Birmingham. Had Ilsley secured this addition after being shown the letter of 12 June? If so, was that why those seven words were added?[22]

❧

Before then had occurred the ordeal of the Hampson will case. A wealthy Catholic widow had died leaving £8000 to the Sisters of Charity, whereupon the Benedictines of Ampleforth advanced a counter-claim to some of the money. They eventually withdrew, only to open the way to a niece of the deceased, who alleged that the Sisters had exercised undue pressure on her aunt and was bent on testing, successfully, as it proved, her claim in the courts. Further details of this lamentable affair and the toll it took of Mother Geneviève and the community, both emotionally and financially, need not be repeated here. The relevant fact for us is that Bishop Ilsley, like Rome, wanted a compromise to be quickly agreed by the parties without recourse to the civil courts and was often unsympathetic to the Sisters, though generous and impartial enough to acknowledge towards the end that at least part of Mother Geneviève's case was 'stronger than I was prepared to find [initially].'

However, when Fr Sole wrote an account in 1892 of what became a *cause célèbre*, entitled 'Selly Park Convent and the Hampson Will Case', and then Mother Geneviève ordered superiors of branch houses to read it to their communities, Bishop Ilsley was irate. 'I had thought of directly countermanding this mischievous order', he wrote, 'which I strongly condemn', but instead he now required Mother Dupuis herself to withdraw it and to forbid the houses to retain any copies in their possession, 'which I consider to be injurious to the interests of peace and charity, not to say justice.' His command was obeyed.

Later Mother Geneviève would make the following formal statement about the whole unhappy affair:

'I have never disobeyed the Bishop in any matter in which he had a right of command, all assertions to the contrary notwithstanding. His advice, I am sorry to say, I have not always been able at all times to follow.'[23]

That declaration deserves careful re-reading. Every phrase has been carefully weighed and no doubt re-written several times - to combine due deference with firmness.

The Hampson case inevitably implicated the Archbishop of Westminster and was soon reported to

Propaganda. As far as relations between Bishop Ilsley and Mother Geneviève were concerned, it led from bad to worse. We depend for the subsequent story on Fr Sole, perhaps a man of somewhat explosive temperament, and we must remember that we are hearing only his side of the cause. He tells a rather unedifying story.

Thus he wrote of the damage which could result from the 'estrangement' which left her isolated. 'Ten years of strife' between her and the bishop had come to an end, Sole concluded, with the Decree of 1898, 'so pronounced and strong and lofty (it was) in tone, wiping out with a blessed sponge the signs and memories (of conflict).' But the bishop had allegedly used his influence in Rome against her and 'did not at all like being confronted with his misrepresentations of you ... this gives you a great power with the Sacred Congregation', he judged.[24]

In 1894 Mother Geneviève had complained to Propaganda about the bishop's reluctance to return papers 'belonging to your archives', despite repeated requests. When the Decree of 1898 and its accompanying Animadversions were sent to him a new tussle ensued, because he either failed or refused to send Mother Dupuis the original Latin texts. Fr Sole believed that this was because he wanted to be in control of re-writing the Rule to meet Rome's requirements and to recover influence over the order for himself.

Mother Geneviève was strongly opposed to the idea of provinces and had told Ilsley so years before. He had replied that her 'alarm' was 'absolutely groundless'. In the event he was wrong; and Mother Geneviève may well have feared that, given his strong 'romanitas', he would force the issue. She wanted to remain under the Congregation for Bishops and Regulars (in part because English bishops dealt with Propaganda?). He wanted her to be subject to Propaganda. Then there was another point of friction. Mother Geneviève was determined to build a worthy chapel and infirmary at Selly Park before she died. How much say would the bishop have in this? Would he be able to control the plans? Fr Sole was adamant. 'Signify to the Bishop that you are going to build [i.e. whatever happens] and ask for his approbation in the normal way,' he counselled. But, as the order was under Bishops and Regulars, the bishop must 'mind his ps and qs. I question very much whether you have to show him the plans ... I should not do so unless requested.'[25]

And now there was a new confrontation concerning access to the original Latin document sent from Rome in 1898. Fr Sole repeatedly urged Mother Geneviève to force the bishop's hand. He even telegraphed a suitable bid : 'Will your Lordship send me by earliest post the Latin text?', and added, 'use not a word more'. She must keep on asking for the document. 'If he still will not send it he will be made to do so.' Later he could say, 'Please, Ma Mère', say to him 'with profound respect' that you request that the papers be sent without further delay and would have to inform Rome if he still persisted in withholding them. 'His Lordship', Sole judged, was 'on the tack of wearing you out ... He is out of the Decree [i.e. was not mentioned in it] and feels it ... he is straining to death his legitimate powers. But they know him in Rome and any encroachment on his side will most certainly be checked.' A few days later (6 April 1898) he was writing : 'Nothing will ever be done spontaneously in your cause, which is God's cause, by his Lordship.' And Sole suggested further that Mother Geneviève should ask Rome to nominate a cardinal-protector for her order.

The immediate outcome of this fracas is unknown. Mother Dupuis was now very aged and frail. She was too ill to attend the General Chapter of 1900 in person. Bishop Ilsley again presided and, we must presume, with his support if not on his initiative, it was agreed to accept the division of the community into provinces. Three Sisters were deputed to prepare a scheme. On the following day, 11 July, a plan to set up four provinces consisting of 14, 14, 12, and 12 branch houses respectively was passed.[26]

Presumably because this was fundamentally alien to the foundress's wishes (and no doubt many others') the decision to 'provincialise' was not executed. Shortly before the next Triennial General Council, of 1903, met, Mother Geneviève had resigned (and died a holy death on the following 25 September, surrounded by many Sisters). So the Chapter that foregathered on 28 July 1903 had election of the new superior general on its agenda. It was obviously a fraught occasion. Following the decision made three years earlier, those attending should have been the provincials and provincial delegates. Instead, they were the usual superioresses of branch houses. As Bishop Ilsley conceded, this was an 'apparent irregularity'. Furthermore, there are two sets of minutes of that meeting in the official record. The first recorded that the Council had decided that with 'an active Mother General the important work of visitation of branch houses can easily be carried by herself or one of her Assistants, and that it is neither desirable or necessary, for the present, to divide the Community into provinces.' It is not clear when this conclusion was reached, but it helps us to understand why nothing had been done to implement the previous General Chapter's decision. But this entry is crossed out in the minute book and instead it is recorded that, after the election of a new superior general, it was resolved 'that the Sacred Congregation be petitioned to grant a delay in the establishment of Provinces.'

What had happened? The likeliest explanation (but which can only be surmise) is that the decision to accept provinces was promoted by the bishop, that it was unwelcome to the Sisters as a whole and that, as soon as it was possible to foresee the arrival of an active superior general (whose appointment would remove one of the reasons for a federal structure) the Council took it upon itself to quash the plan. Bishop Ilsley would no doubt have regarded this action as *ultra vires*. What battles then ensued we will never know. But the upshot was that Rome was to be petitioned to grant 'a delay' in the implementation of the plan agreed three years previously.[27]

Three years later revised Constitutions were discussed again prior to submission to Bishops and Regulars. As we shall see, by now a serious controversy was developing in the order concerning not only some recent amendments to the Constitution which were regarded as harsh by some, but also the larger question of the rights of professed Sisters to participate in the governance of the Congregation. This in turn produced an Extraordinary General Chapter in 1907 because

Bishops and Regulars ruled that the proceedings of 1906 were invalid - since they had been conducted under the misapprehension that the decisions of 1900 had been overtaken by later events and had lapsed, which, Rome ruled, they had not. As a result, the proceedings of the 1906 General Chapter concerning the Constitutions (as the Rule was now regularly called) were unanimously rescinded; whereupon the bishop withdrew from the meeting - interestingly - and under Mother General's guidance the assembly resolved to petition the Holy See to allow General Chapters, 'so long as the Congregation is not divided into provinces', to consist of superiors of all larger houses (plus one delegate apiece) and two representatives from groups of smaller houses. 'When the Congregation is divided into provinces', it was agreed, provincials and two delegates from every province would attend. So a compromise had emerged : the unity of the order had been preserved for the immediate future, but provinces might still be set up eventually.

Negotiations with Rome for final approbation were to drag on for many more years. New 'Observations' proposed by a consultor to the Sacred Congregation were discussed at the eighth General Chapter in 1909 and in 1910 Rome did indeed give its approval - but only for a trial period - to the revised

"My Dear Reverend Mother..."

'To send away three novices at once is a big thing ... you have your reasons and three very good reasons ... If there is no scandal, I pray you to have great patience. There is early fruit and there is fruit that matures late. It would be a bad calculation to reject a tree because its fruit does not ripen with that of others.'
- *Père Compagnon, Chartres, 1 November 1853*

Right: St. John's Priory, Banbury

Constitutions. Then came the major revision of the whole of Canon Law, published in 1916, which necessitated further re-thinking and re-writing of details by the Sisters. A third Extraordinary General Chapter in 1928 at last approved a final text for submission to Rome. Two years later the General Chapter was told that the priest who was revising (yet again!) the Constitutions for the Sacred Congregation was hopeful that approval would come 'after a short time'. It also heard that Rome had granted a cardinal-protector, thirty years after Fr Sole had first suggested the need for one.

At last, on 24 March 1931, Rome gave its final and definitive judgment on the Rule, i.e. Constitutions, 70 years after Mother Geneviève had first embarked on her quest for papal approval. Bishop Ilsley was dead. The idea of provinces had been laid to rest - except that, at the 17th Ordinary General Chapter in July 1965 it was revived once more. It was defeated by 63 votes to 1, while permission to wear wrist-watches, refused in 1959, was carried by 64 votes to none. Mother Geneviève, who was forward-looking as well as devoted to maintaining the unity of her spiritual family, would have approved of both votes.[28]

NOTES

Unless otherwise indicated, all references are to materials in the Convent Archives, Selly Park, Birmingham.

1. W. J. Battersby, 'Educational Work of the Religious Orders of Women, 1850-1950' in G.A.Beck (ed.), The English Catholics, 1850-1950
2. George V. Hudson, Mother Geneviève Dupuis (1923), p 57
3. Box 3 / 61, bundle I. Hudson, op.cit., pp 60-71
4. Box 16 / 184
5. Box 2 / 54, 55, 57, 63; 3 / 67; 1 / 19
6. Box 2 / 51; 38 / 14
7. Archdiocese of Birmingham Archives, B 1311
8. Box 4 / 68
9. Box 4 / 68
10. Box 21 / 212
11. Box 3 / 67
12. Box 38 / 296 / 5, 7. 11
13. Box 38 / 296 / 5
14. Box 38 / 296 / 14
15. Box 38 / 236 / 15
16. Box 38 / 296 / 9
17. Box 38 / 296 / 19
18. Box 1 / 46
19. Box 4 / 68
20. Printed in full in Hudson, op. cit., pp 222-4 and (Latin text) 321-2
21. Box 40 / 21
22. Box 1 / 40
23. Box 1 / 89
24. Box 6 / 87-89
25. Box 39 / 300
26. Box 39 / 300; 4 / 69
27. Box 44 / 328, Record of General Chapters, June 1888-1924
28. For all the above see Ibid., 1903, 1906-7

*Statue of
St. Geneviève in the
garden at Selly Park*

Diocesan Map - England & Wales

Birmingham
Aston Hall, Atherstone, Avon Dassett, Banbury, Besford Court, Brewood, Cheadle, Church Enstone, Croome Court, Dudley, Heronbrook, Kidderminster, Leamington, Longton, Newbold Revel, Oakamoor, Oldbury, Princethorpe, Radford, Sambourne, Solihull, Spetchley, Stourbridge, Studley, Sutton Coldfield, Walsall, Wednesbury, West Bromwich, Worcester

Coleshill
St. Edward's, St. Gerard's, St. Joan's, St. Paul's

Coventry
Corpus Christi, Holy Family, St. Mary's, St. Paul's

City of Birmingham
Annie Bright Weston House, Archbishop's House, Beechenhurst, Billesley, Cathedral House, Erdington, Great Barr, Handsworth (St. Augustine's, St. Joseph's, St. Paul's), Harborne, Highgate, Maryvale Centre, Nechells, Northfield, Olton, Selly Park, Smethwick, St. Catherine's, St. Chad's, St. Michael's, Vernon Road (St. Paul's), St. Vincent's, University Chaplaincy, West Indian Chaplaincy, Woodville

Leeds
Batley, Birstall, Goole, Ripon, Selby, Shipley

Bradford
Girlington, Heaton Mount, Manningham, (St. Cuthbert's, St. Joseph's) St. Mary's, St. Patrick's

City of Leeds
Headingley, Moor Drive, St. Anne's, St. Augustine's, St. Patrick's

Wakefield
Our Lady's, St. Paul's, St. Joseph's

Liverpool
Appleton, Ashton-in-Makerfield, Billinge, Crosby, Ditton, Formby, Gillmoss, Penketh, Rainhill, Prescot, Southport (St. Marie's, St. Patrick's), Standish, Sutton Manor, Lydiate, Warrington (Sacred Heart, St. Joseph's)

City of Liverpool
Archbishop's House, Great Mersey St., Wavertree, Woolton

Cardiff
Abergavenny, Belmont, Llanarth

Clifton
Bath, Cheltenham, Chipping Campden, Taunton, Woodchester

Plymouth
Axminster, Buckfast, Dawlish, Keyham, Parkstone, Wimborne

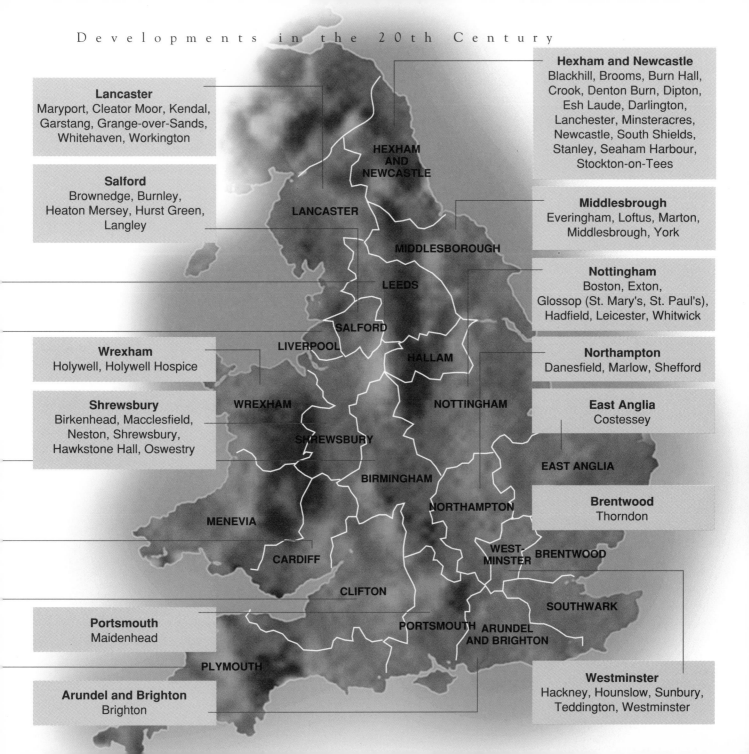

Hexham and Newcastle
Blackhill, Brooms, Burn Hall, Crook, Denton Burn, Dipton, Esh Laude, Darlington, Lanchester, Minsteracres, Newcastle, South Shields, Stanley, Seaham Harbour, Stockton-on-Tees

Lancaster
Maryport, Cleator Moor, Kendal, Garstang, Grange-over-Sands, Whitehaven, Workington

Middlesbrough
Everingham, Loftus, Marton, Middlesbrough, York

Salford
Brownedge, Burnley, Heaton Mersey, Hurst Green, Langley

Nottingham
Boston, Exton, Glossop (St. Mary's, St. Paul's), Hadfield, Leicester, Whitwick

Northampton
Danesfield, Marlow, Shefford

Wrexham
Holywell, Holywell Hospice

East Anglia
Costessey

Shrewsbury
Birkenhead, Macclesfield, Neston, Shrewsbury, Hawkstone Hall, Oswestry

Brentwood
Thorndon

Portsmouth
Maidenhead

Westminster
Hackney, Hounslow, Sunbury, Teddington, Westminster

Arundel and Brighton
Brighton

Map labels: HEXHAM AND NEWCASTLE, LANCASTER, MIDDLESBOROUGH, LEEDS, SALFORD, LIVERPOOL, HALLAM, WREXHAM, NOTTINGHAM, SHREWSBURY, MENEVIA, BIRMINGHAM, CARDIFF, NORTHAMPTON, EAST ANGLIA, WEST-MINSTER, BRENTWOOD, CLIFTON, SOUTHWARK, PORTSMOUTH, ARUNDEL AND BRIGHTON, PLYMOUTH

Developments in the Twentieth Century

Uncertain Years

The death of a founder or foundress of an order can rarely fail to send shock-waves throughout the community concerned. This would be especially true when the foundress was as long-lived, strongwilled and charismatic as Mother Geneviève. Who could possibly be an adequate successor? Would she be able to hold the Congregation together and revivify it? What changes would she promote or allow? Mother Foundress had exercised unique authority, for forty years without Assistants, a Council or General Chapter, which was virtually unquestionable as well as unquestioned.

How would her successor interpret her role? What hitherto hidden hopes and aspirations might now break the surface? What new challenges and opportunities awaited? Things would inevitably be different. But in what ways, and how?

True, Mother Geneviève had been seriously unwell for many years - and bedridden for about three - before she died. So the Congregation had had time to prepare for that moment when the Foundress completed her earthly pilgrimage. Moreover, there had been only one new foundation in the last decade[1], a fact which helped to prepare the Sisters for the inevitability of a new beginning, or at least a new chapter in their history. But no one could have foreseen that Mother Geneviève's successor, Mother Gabriel, would herself die less than six months after her election. This was indeed a grievous blow. Furthermore, the third superior general, Mothert Benedicta Brodhurst, held office for only three years, so it was not until the long and prosperous generalship of Mother Mecthilde Thelen that the Congregation's stability was fully restored. And in the meantime the Sisters had weathered a few storms. In the first place, the question of whether to establish provinces still loomed. Secondly, the Rule was still not finally approved and frequent revision, to take account of changing circumstances, could cause sometimes sharp differences of view. Thirdly, by 1906 a clear division of opinion had emerged among the Sisters concerning the term of office of superiors of branch houses and their place in General Chapters. Should they be appointed for no more than three years (and not be re-appointed until a further three years had elapsed) and should they have an *ex officio* right of attending and voting at General Chapters?

At the General Chapter of 1906 those who had pressed for the three-year term of office and 'open' election by branch houses of their delegates carried the day. However, shortly afterwards, cooler counsels prevailed. Triennial appointment of superiors, accompanied by automatic removal from office, would be gravely disruptive of the lives of houses and 'disastrous to Catholic education', a petition from superiors declared, and 'would end in Sisters losing their position in and hold of schools.[2] So, following intervention by Bishop Ilsley and appeal to Rome, an Extraordinary Chapter in 1907 unanimously agreed to rescind the proceedings of the Chapter of the previous year 'regarding the recently drafted Constitutions' and to reinstate the Constitutions of 1900 - but with the important concession that every house with 12 or more members would be represented at the General Chapter by the superior and one elected delegate. Smaller houses were to be grouped together and to elect two delegates apiece.[3]

The four years since the death of Mother Foundress had been unsettled ones. Nonetheless they had seen eight new foundations, including the first in Ireland and the beginning of the Congregation's involvement in Coleshill, all of which paved the way for six decades of confident expansion and diversification of service to the Church.

"My Dear Reverend Mother..."

'You are poor, may you always be poor, and your subjects worthy of poverty; for material prosperity is a bad augury for spiritual success. You are persecuted ... May you always be persecuted, it is the mark of a work of God.'
- *Père Compagnon, Chartres,*
29 January 1850

Education Expanded

The Congregation's primary ministry continued to consist in staffing parish schools, parish visiting, teaching the Faith to adults and contributing in many other ways to parish life. But teaching the poor remained its chief apostolate. In the mid-nineteenth century elementary education was not compulsory and poor or working class children were lucky if the Churches or voluntary societies provided for them. True, in 1839 some government grants became available and in 1846 the Catholic Poor School Committee was founded to promote Catholic education and to claim whatever grants they could. At about the same time the Factory Act of 1844 attempted to limit the employment hours of children and to insist on children between the ages of eight and thirteen spending three days or six half-days in school. These were the "half-timers". This was the situation into which Mother Geneviève came. In Banbury she opened night schools for children working during the day. She also insisted on her Sisters being trained as well as possible and there are many references to the number of "certificated" and "uncertificated" teachers she would send to a mission. From 1853 there was a Training School for Catholic teachers at St. Chad's as well as the one for Sisters at Banbury - to train Sisters to teach in parish elementary schools.

The twentieth century was quickly to see the educational work of the Congregation undergo fast expansion.

First came involvement in secondary education. Encouraged by the Education Act of 1902, which empowered local authorities to provide secondary education for elementary school children, Bishop Ilsley turned to the Sisters and asked them to build and equip a secondary school for Catholic girls of Birmingham and the surrounding area. Thus did St. Paul's School for Girls, Vernon Road, Edgbaston - a major new venture - come about. It was built by the Congregation at a cost of £12,000. Donations amounted to a mere £279! It opened on 7 October 1908, and still serves the needs of Catholic families of Britain's second largest city, having survived all the educational changes of recent decades and become a Catholic comprehensive school for girls.

A momentous step had been taken. Other secondary schools soon followed, some of them, like Holywell (first founded in 1859) and Kilfinane (opened in 1903) growing out of existing small independent schools. Later secondary schools opened at Sunbury (1926), Wimborne (1930) and Kilmallock (1933). A secondary school in Leicester was taken over from the Nativity Sisters in 1955 and Greenhills (Dublin)

Right: Selly Park.
St. Edward's Primary School.

Dudley. St. Joseph's School.
(no date).

opened in 1964. In the meantime, three secondary schools had been opened in South Africa: Modimong and Zeerust in 1954 and Rustenburg in 1963. Sisters had also been teaching in diocesan secondary schools throughout Britain, often looking after the senior pupils of schools which had begun as parochial primary schools. Over the years, therefore, the Sisters have provided thousands of Catholic pupils with a secondary education.

Mother Geneviève had long wanted to establish a training centre for teachers, both laywomen and her religious. In 1901 the first step towards this goal was taken when a former warehouse in Whittall Street in Birmingham opened as a centre for teacher-training. Nine years later a training college was established at Selly Park itself which, remarkably, from 1912 to 1927 had a laywoman, Miss Constance Fox, as its principal. By 1914, it could accommodate 40 students. It was not a residential college. The student Sisters continued to live in the convent at Selly Park and the laywomen in a house nearby (Beechenhurst). Although the college was successful and satisfied the requirements of the Board of Education, the Board refused to give grants or allow the college to increase its numbers until the case was taken to Parliament and grants were given from 1927. The Congregation had borne all the costs until then.

Right: Mother Ignatius Caley. She was the first superior in Kilfinane from 1903 to 1918, when she was appointed novice mistress, the post she held until 1931.

St. Paul's College, Newbold Revel.

The intention had been to build a new teacher training college in Birmingham, but the outbreak of the Second World War prevented this. Instead, the college evacuated to Woodchester in Gloucester and after the war moved to its final site at Newbold Revel, a splendid stately home in rural Warwickshire. Here, until its closure in 1978, the Sisters ran a thriving teacher-training college which produced hundreds of Catholic teachers, many of whom are still working in schools all over the country.

Today the situation has changed. The Congregation is no longer involved in tertiary education in England although it retains an involvement in Mankwe Christian College in South Africa. The participation in secondary education in England has also diminished, but the Sisters still run St. Paul's, Vernon Road, and one Sister teaches in a diocesan school - St. Joseph's School in Workington. In South Africa St. Anne's High School, Modimong, has been handed over to the Sisters of St. Brigid and one Sister teaches in a Catholic secondary school in Bapong. In Ireland, the three secondary schools still flourish.

The commitment to primary education, however, continues in four countries. Currently, Sisters are teaching in fifteen schools in England, two in Ireland and one in South Africa. In Romania they teach in two 'first schools' and in a developing primary school.

To Ireland

It is an interesting fact that while, from early days, many Sisters had come from Ireland, the Congregation did not have a convent there until Kilfinane opened in 1903. The project was in hand before the death of Mother Foundress. She had been opposed to the idea of extending the Congregation's work to Ireland on the ground that there were already enough Sisters and orders at work there, but eventually changed her mind. We have evidence that the idea was discussed at the July 1903 General Chapter. One account spoke of the Congregation extending its work to Ireland "in compliance with the wishes of the bishops there and with full approval of his Lordship the Bishop of Birmingham." Plans were well advanced by the time of Mother Foundress' death on 25 September, 1903.

Kilfinane convent opened on 15 October 1903, the plan being to take over an existing National school and eventually to establish a secondary school as well - and to visit the sick. The great generosity of local people from the time of the Sisters' arrival enabled the school to be enlarged and then re-built after it was burned down in 1908. Parish collections and donations, together with grants from the National Board and the Congregation itself enabled the buildings to be completed. Bishop O'Dwyer himself made a significant contribution, including payment for the chapel fittings.

Thus was the Congregation's first venture into Ireland accomplished. The school flourished (and

IRELAND

Dublin, Greenhills
Blackrock

Limerick
Kilmallock
Kilfinane

Clonakilty

still flourishes). An initial roll of 90 had increased to 220 by 1928, when the secondary school was added, and boarding facilities made available to meet the needs of the pupils drawn from a population scattered over a large area. The school became co-educational in 1968 and the handsome new Scoil Pól was built in 1987 with Congregational funds, grants and much local fundraising.

The foundation in Kilfinane prepared the way for others. In 1927 the Sisters arrived in Kilmallock and took charge of a girls' primary school in Wolfe Tone St. and taught a few private pupils in Sarsfield St. A new primary school was built in 1929 and by 1933 St. Joseph's Convent which included the Secondary School was completed. Boarding facilities were added and it later became co-educational. In 1991 the entire building was reconstructed as a school, with funding from the Congregation, the Parents' Association and other donors.

Both these schools not only made a significant contribution to Irish education; they also produced a large number of young women who subsequently entered the Congregation. Like all Sisters before and since they entered at the Mother House. But during the Second World War Kilmallock served as a temporary novitiate until Sisters were able to travel once more to Selly park. In 1964, a primary school and a secondary school were established on the outskirts of Dublin at Greenhills, to serve the needs of the growing population in suburban housing estates such as Tallaght. A new convent and church were subsequently built on the campus. Both schools became popular with large numbers of pupils, so extensions were soon necessary

Thus the ministry of primary and secondary education remains as strong today in the Congregation's schools in Ireland as when they first began. However, the way in which it is continued is changing, as is indicated by the appointment in 1993 of the first "lay" principal in Greenhills Secondary School.

As in England, other apostolates developed. Archbishop McQuaid of Dublin, who encouraged the building of Greenhills, was a Holy Ghost Father who had known the Sisters from Blackrock College, where the Congregation had been asked to share in a new type of collaborative ministry. Four Sisters had been sent to the Holy Ghost Fathers' College for boys in 1934 to supervise the kitchen, the infirmary, the linen room and the dormitories. Thus they were able to influence and give a woman's care and love to generations of Blackrock schoolboys. This apostolate continued for over sixty years until 1995.

A further development took place in 1956 with the establishment of Bushmount, Clonakilty, for the care of elderly priests and others. Over the years it was extensively rebuilt and now reaches the high standard demanded for its official registration as a nursing home. As another service to the Church, Sisters ran the household of the Bishop of Limerick from 1979 to 1995.

Today, therefore, the Sisters in the four remaining houses in Ireland are involved in two primary schools, three secondary schools and a nursing home. Their ministry and their presence are as valuable in the changing circumstances of today's world as they were nearly a hundred years ago.

Child Care: Father Hudson's Homes

In the Congregation's heyday in the mid-twentieth century, several hundred Sisters were involved in primary, secondary and tertiary education, and scores more in a wide variety of ministries ranging from care of the elderly to running bishops' households. But the largest single institution to which the Congregation was committed was that most remarkable enterprise, the diocese of Birmingham's Child Rescue Society which still bears the name of its chief architect, Father George V. Hudson. His was one of the most ambitious undertakings of its kind to be found anywhere in the Catholic world; and over the decades hundreds of Sisters of the Congregation of Sisters of Charity of St. Paul helped to sustain its heroic work.

The Sisters' involvement in child care had actually begun during the time of Mother Geneviève, long before the diocesan Rescue Society was founded, when a small orphanage was opened in Radford, Oxfordshire in 1854. A generous local lady donated the house and ground. Later a Mr and Mrs Thomas Perry gave a house in Avon Dassett, Warwickshire, to be used as an orphanage also. So two small orphanages were being run by the Sisters.

Left: (Top) Kilfinane Convent (Middle) Kilmallock Convent (Bottom) Opening of Bushmount, Clonakilty. 16th March 1956.

It was Cardinal Manning, second archbishop of Westminster, who launched the diocesan child rescue movement which became a major feature of Catholic life in Britain. Horrified by the number of Catholic children in the workhouses, Manning, a dedicated campaigner for social justice, set up houses for Catholic children and Poor Law schools. Other bishops follwed his lead, including Bishop Ullathorne, who opened his first Poor Law school, St. Paul's Home for Boys, in Coleshill in 1884 and put it in the care of Mother Geneviève. The Birmingham Diocesan Rescue Society was founded in 1902 by Bishop Ilsley, and Fr Hudson appointed its first secretary.

From the beginning, the Birmingham Diocesan Rescue work was shared by several Congregations of religious, groups of lay people and individuals, and was an example of collaboration at its best. The story of the involvement of the Sisters of St. Paul is thus a part of a larger picture. By 1903 there were five homes in the diocese, including St. Paul's Home in Coleshill. The vision of Father Hudson was of a children's "garden city" at Coleshill. This began with the building of the new St. Edward's Home for boys, which opened in 1906. Mother General was only too willing to give, at the bishop's request, four Sisters for this work. Thus began the long commitment of the Sisters of St. Paul to Father Hudson's Homes. It is

Left: Father Hudson's Homes, Coleshill. St. Edward's Home. Mgr. George Hudson with the boys.

"My Dear Reverend Mother..."

'Your dear Rev. Mother was a wonder on this poor earth of ours, and her work is lasting out bravely after she has gone to her reward. I shall ever look back upon the day I introduced the Sisters in this part of our dear English land as a most blessed one.'

- *Thomas Wilkinson, bishop of Hexham and Newcastle, 1905*

CANADA

OTTAWA

the Congregation's part of this picture which is now described. St. Paul's continued as a boys' home and nursery for small boys until 1925. The building later housed the Physiotherapy School and in 1940 became a girls' home run by Sisters of St. Paul. Later it became a mother and baby home. St. Edward's Home for boys opened in 1906, and was not closed until 1981, by which time over six and a half thousand boys had lived there. The Cottage Homes for younger boys opened in 1925. Alas, these homes closed in 1979. Meanwhile girls had been accommodated in St. Joan's Home, which opened in 1931 and was modern, well-equipped and beautifully furnished and decorated.

At the same time as the opening of St. Edward's, the Sisters became part of a new venture in Canada. For thirty years Canada had been giving homes and work to immigrant youngsters. In 1904 the existing emigration societies amalgamated to form one Catholic Emigration Society with Father Hudson as its secretary. The receiving home for children was St. George's Home, Ottawa, and the Sisters of St. Paul were asked to take charge in 1907. The first superior is buried there, having served for twenty years. The Sisters were responsible for the placing, visiting and well-being of the young people, who regarded St. George's as "home". The mission ended in 1935 with the decrease in employment opportunities for both Canadian and immigrant youth.

In 1913 Fr Hudson had launched another initiative - St. Gerard's Hospital. This boys' infirmary expanded to include orthopaedic nursing for the treatment of children crippled by disease, injury and congenital defects, including tuberculosis and poliomyelitis. This was further extended between 1920 and 1939 to include surgery on hips and spines. Thus was launched one of the earliest hospitals dedicated to the caring of children. Then a School of Nursing was established to train orthopaedic nurses and a Physiotherapy School together with a School of Domestic Science. These schools trained Sisters and young women, many of whom afterwards joined the Congregation. Sisters also travelled from St. Gerard's to hold clinics in the surrounding small towns of Warwickshire and Leicestershire. So Coleshill became the centre of medical 'missionary' work in the Midlands as well as a rich source of postulants to the order.

An unusual apostolate developed between 1936 and 1947 with the hop-pickers in the Herefordshire and Worcestershire hopfields. The Sisters accompanied priests and clerical students to set up a pastoral ministry with the workers, the Sisters looking after all the medical and health requirements.

Education was an important feature of St. Gerard's Hospital when in 1919, the Sisters started teaching children on the wards. This hospital Special School was recognised by the Board of Education. There had always been a school for boys attached to St. Paul's Boys' Home and the Sisters taught there, but in 1915, a school for younger boys was established in St. Edward's Home. This became St. Edward's Primary School in 1925 and included Catholic children from the surrounding area. Many Sisters taught in this school. In 1925 the old school became St. Paul's Central School, providing secondary education for the local pupils.

At the same time the archdiocese was making provision for children with special needs. In 1916 Besford Court School was established for such boys. This was also a home for the boys, since the Sisters looked after the younger boys as boarders and taught them in school. In establishing such a school, the archdiocese was well ahead of its time. The school provided, in a residential setting, care, education and training in practical skills to enable the boys to take their place in society. In 1939 the Sisters and younger boys moved to Sambourne, the older boys remaining in Besford. In 1950 they moved again to the stately home of Croome Court, set in spacious parkland. In 1978 the Sisters and the younger boys moved back to Besford Court, to St. Joseph's House, which also

cared for a small number of girls. The school was finally closed by the archdiocese in 1996.

With the new policies on fostering and adoption, the need for institutional child-care diminished and other needs were addressed. So St. Joseph's Home for the Elderly began in 1981 and St. Catherine's House, which in 1983 had been part of a project providing holidays for handicapped young people, opened in 1986 as a long-stay home for those with special needs.

Another aspect of the work of Father Hudson's Homes was the development of mother and baby homes. The Sisters of St. Paul were involved in this work from 1943 to 1973 at Woodville in Raddlebarn Road, Selly Park, a home established in 1915 by a branch of the Catholic Women's League. Later, when it became St. Mary's Hospice, Sisters were initially involved.

The Congregation also undertook child care in other dioceses. In 1907, at the request of Father Berry, four Sisters were sent to staff Our Lady's Home, Greenfield House in Billinge in the Liverpool Diocese. The Sisters also staffed St. Mary's School in Billinge. In 1962 the Sisters and children moved to Newstead, in Wavertree, Liverpool where they stayed until 1982, when this type of care was no longer required. Liverpool was also the scene of another

"*My Dear Reverend Mother...*"

'You and your Congregation are the grain of mustard that God has thrown on a land once so fertile and for 300 years stricken by the barrenness of heresy.'
- Mgr Clausel de Montals, bishop of Chartres, 5 March 1849

early venture. In 1907 four Sisters were sent to take charge of what was known as the Industrial School attached to St. Joseph's Home for Boys, Great Mersey Street, where the previous teachers had all been male. They remained here until the reorganisation in 1922.

Northampton Diocese also had Sisters of St. Paul in St. Francis' Home, Shefford in Bedfordshire from 1919 until 1944. Two recent foundations were a mother and baby home and a children's home in Headingley, Leeds, which functioned from 1976 to 1984, and a family home in South Shields which ran from 1981 to 1989.

To South Africa

Fifty years after the Sisters of St. Paul opened their first house in Ireland came an invitation to venture much further afield - when a request arrived from Archbishop Garner of Pretoria to work in his diocese. Here was a major new challenge. The General Chapter of 1954 was consulted and its mandate given for the first mission outside Europe since the Sisters had taken on St. George's Home in Ottawa nearly fifty years previously.

The first group of Sisters arrived in South Africa in Autumn 1954, and was followed by a second, at the end of the year. The two groups celebrated Christmas together in the first branch convent in South Africa, St. Mary's, Zeerust, where a school was established. The Sisters also helped with the pastoral work of the priest in the surrounding area. This apostolate was to continue for sixteen years until 1970, when the school closed.

Just after that first Christmas in Zeerust, on 30 December, 1954, Modimong, "God's own place", was officially opened. Here the ministry was among the black South African people, working with the Redemptorist Fathers already living there. A primary school and a high school, St. Anne's, were established, most of the secondary pupils being boarders. The mission had been founded on land given to the church by a very generous benefactor, Mrs. Christina Vermaas.

In 1957 a small hospital in Modimong

Modimong. 1950s Lessons

opened with seven male T.B. patients. A larger hospital opened the following year. Despite many difficulties and fears of closure, the hospital grew steadily, thanks to help from Selly Park, donations, grants from the Pretoria Department of Health and a substantial donation from the Knights of Da Gama, which paid for a new block for female patients in 1964. Eventually the hospital was allowed to take general patients and in 1973 a School of Nursing was established and, later, clinics established in the surrounding villages. The hospital was taken over by the Bophutatswana government in 1977.

Something else of great importance also happened at Modimong, namely the founding of a new Congregation of African Sisters, the Sisters of St. Brigid. Archbishop Garner of Pretoria requested that the Sisters of St. Paul found such a

Congregation and train the Sisters until such time as they could become independent. The Archbishop chose their patron, saying that he hoped they would do for their women what St. Brigid had done for the women of Ireland. The Sisters of St. Brigid took over the primary school until its closure and undertook teaching and health care work. They became an autonomous Congregation in 1987 In 1994 the Sisters of St. Paul withdrew from Modimong and the Sisters of St. Brigid took over St. Anne's High School. This was exactly the pioneering, 'enabling' and 'empowering' work of which Mother Foundress would have been proud.

Meanwhile a new foundation had been established in the Republic of South Africa, in the platinum mining town of Rustenburg. The Dominican Sisters had established a primary school in the town and this was

Above: Mrs. Christina Vermaas, who gave the land for the mission in Modimong to the Bishop of Kimberley. Subsequently it came under Pretoria and the Bishop gave it to the Redemptorists. Mrs Vermaas is buried in Modimong.

Left: Rustenburg. Ministry in Boitekong - crèche.

Convent on the outskirts of the town. The convent opened in 1966 and the school was registered in 1967. At first it consisted of a primary and secondary school with boarders. In 1983 it became a primary school only and began to grow as a multi-racial school before the establishment of the new South Africa which abolished the separate homelands and the apartheid policy. A separate department of the primary school and separately registered is the pre-school, or nursery school, which now has over seventy pupils. Sisters from Rustenburg undertook catechetical work in surrounding villages and settlements. This outreach continues today with Sisters working in nursery education in Boitekong and a Sister teaching in Bapong at St. Teresa's High School. Selly Park Convent, Rustenburg, the only South African property owned by the Congregation, has become the main convent for the Sisters of St. Paul in South Africa.

As in Britain, the Congregation's work diversified in response to new needs. Thus Sisters taught and were responsible for catering in the Hammanskraal and Pretoria seminaries, and in the Archbishop's household in Pretoria. A different educational venture, in collaboration with other religious orders, diocesan priests and the Volunteer Missionary Movement, started in 1979 at Phokeng, in Bophutatswana. At the request of Mgr. Hallett, the

Prefect Apostolic of Rustenburg, a convent was established at St. Joseph's Phokeng. Sisters taught in the local African school in Phokeng and in the High School at Tlhabane. In 1980 the Phokeng project was set up to teach basic skills. In 1990 the main project was handed over to the Government and to the diocese.

Thirty years after the initial Chapter mandate was given to go to South Africa, Bishop Naidoo of Cape Town asked for Sisters to train and support volunteer catechists, the majority being from disadvantaged areas throughout the Archdiocese. Sisters began work in 1988 in this diocese, many miles from the original Transvaal foundations. At the time, there were about twelve hundred catechists in the diocese serving ninety two parishes. Each parish catered for a weekly average of five hundred children. This was actually Cape Town's third effort to secure the services of the Sisters of St. Paul. Archbishop Leonard had made a request to Mother Geneviève as long ago as 1877 and Bishop Naidoo had previously asked in 1977. The 1990s were to see the Sisters involved in two new ventures in South Africa. First, in 1991 they became involved in Mankwe Christian College and in 1992 Holy Family Primary School. Neither establishment is owned by the Congregation. Both are examples of collaborative ministry, involving the Sisters, other religious and lay people.

Right: Rustenburg.
Selly Park Convent.

Mogwase. Holy Family
Primary School.

SCOTLAND

Glasgow

Musselburgh

Galashiels

Birnie Knowe

Care of the Elderly

In 1907, whilst the Congregation's involvement in education and child care was expanding fast, the Congregation was requested to care for the elderly at St. Anne's, Musselburgh, Scotland. St. Anne's became home for many retired priests. Now, with a new building, it provides for thirty-nine elderly women and men. At the request of the Birmingham Archdiocese the Congregation was asked to take over the running of Annie Bright Weston House in 1953 and in 1962 a home for retired priests at Aston Hall. A similar home had already been opened in 1956 at Clonakilty, Cork. These three homes continue to thrive. Sisters also cared for the elderly in St. Joseph's Home, Coleshill, and in sheltered accommodation in Olton (1979 - 1983), in Harborne (1979 - 1993) and in Oldbury (1986 1993). Of continuing importance to the Congregation is the care of the elderly Sisters in Selly Park Nursing Home, now a registered Home, but still called affectionately "The Infirmary." From the time of Mother Geneviève sick and elderly Sisters came home to Selly Park for nursing care. She built the first infirmary in the 1890s and it is still in use. In 1932 the new modern infirmary was completed. Here elderly Sisters and those recuperating from illness or operations receive the best medical and nursing care, and at the same time join in the daily prayer life of the Mother House. Here are many faithful women of wisdom who have worked hard in the Lord's vineyard. It is a privileged place.

Further Diversification

Reflecting on these twentieth-century developments, we can see that the major developments in ministry, namely secondary and tertiary education, child care and care of the elderly grew directly out of the original mission to care for the poor and educate children. Similarly the developments in Ireland and in South Africa followed a similar pattern to that in Britain. Inherent in the original aims of the Congregation, was a general intention to care for the poor and to assist priests and bishops in their ministry. Consequently, the Congregation has always been willing to listen to a request from the Church and, if possible, to accede to requests. Sometimes, for various reasons, this has not been possible. However, throughout the twentieth century, there has been an increasing diversification of ministry, sometimes the beginning of long-term apostolates, sometimes temporary or short-term. Some of the new ministries have developed from previous work and some are new ventures.

Parish Ministry

There has been a significant change in the Parish apostolates in that in many places a Sister is designated "Parish Sister" with responsibility for Parish programmes and in other places this is the sole ministry of the convent, there being no Sisters in school. This work began and still continues in Warrington from 1982, in Maidenhead and in Billesley from 1988. Sisters worked in Wakefield from 1990 until 1995. From 1996 Sisters are working from a new diocesan house in Warrington.

Catechetics

Sisters began to work with diocesan catechetical teams soon after Vatican II. This is a collaborative, team ministry, empowering people over a wide area. Sisters have worked in Birmingham and Plymouth and are now working in the dioceses of Leeds, Southwark and Cape Town, South Africa.

Collaborative Ministry with other Religious

The first such ministries concerned educational establishments. In 1934 the Sisters took over the domestic arrangements and the infirmary for the boys at Blackrock College in Dublin. This service lasted until 1995. One Sister continues to teach in the junior school there. Sisters also taught and took charge of the infirmary at Princethorpe College, Rugby from 1978 until 1987. These were joint ministries with other religious orders. Similar collaboration took place with Sisters working in retreat and conference centres: Minsteracres from 1976, Maryvale from 1980, Hawkestone Hall from 1983 until 1988, Burn Hall from 1986 until 1992 and St. Peter's Pastoral Centre at Glasgow from 1988 until 1993. A similar collaborative ministry had been undertaken during the Second World War and afterwards, when the Sisters staffed various bishops' households. Sisters have served at Westminster, Liverpool, Limerick and Pretoria, and remain at work in Birmingham and Birkenhead.

Retreats

Congregational retreats have always been part of the work at Selly Park and later at Teddington. Today St. Paul's Retreat Centre, Teddington provides a variety of retreats, courses and spiritual direction for religious and lay people in an ecumenical setting. Likewise, St. Martha's Conference Centre in Selly Park provides Congregational retreats and conference facilities for a wide variety of groups and individuals also in an ecumenical spirit.

Chaplaincy, Counselling and Therapeutic Ministries

Chaplaincy work was undertaken at Birmingham University from 1970 until 1990. Individual Sisters have been working at the West Indian Chaplaincy (since 1974) and the Irish Welfare Centre (since 1995) in Birmingham.

The Voice of Geneviève Dupuis

'Love each other in God, bear with each other's shortcomings with true charity'
- *Geneviève Dupuis*

1. **Bucharest**
2. **Câmpulung - Muscel**
   Parohia R.C.
   Novitiate- St. Paul
   Casa - Ieremia Valahul
3. **Motru**
4. **Tirgoviste**

Several Sisters are involved in, or training for, social work, therapy, counselling, family therapy and programmes for people with HIV and AIDS. In 1978 Heronbrook House was opened as a counselling and therapeutic centre for priests and religious. This was a significant ministry, unique at that time in the post-Vatican II era. In 1996 a new programme is being planned to meet the needs of Church and society.

The Fireside Centre

A day centre, with the needs of homeless and needy people in mind, has been established at The Fireside Centre in the heart of Birmingham. This is a collaborative ministry with many volunteers, religious and lay, ecumenical and interfaith in character. The emphasis is on helping individuals to recover their sense of purpose. At the same time many services are provided, including medical help, counselling and advice, refreshments, washing and recreational facilities. Referral to professional agencies is undertaken. Other schemes, such as literacy classes and a crèche are developed as needed.

Associates

The Sisters of St. Paul have always had a tradition of working with other lay people in their ministries. From such co-workers, parents of pupils, friends and others a nascent group of Associates is coming together, to live out their sharing of the charism. Currently there are several groups.

To Romania

Once again, towards the end of the twentieth century another country has called, namely Romania - soon after the collapse of the Communist empire of which it had been part and the overthrow of of its especially harsh regime. Two Sisters, in 1990, felt called to work there. It is a measure of the selfless vitality of the Congregation that both of them had in fact retired. Undaunted they set out on their new apostolate in a strange, torn and terribly impoverished land, first as volunteers with Health Aid U.K. working with babies with AIDS. Later, Sisters worked with the street children under the auspices of CARITAS.

Their zeal and that of other Sisters

and volunteers who came to help them, produced requests from the diocese of Bucharest to run parochial nursery schools and organise summer schools for young people. Sisters took on a parish nursery school in Bucharest and also taught a class in a Communist nursery school. Soon an invitation came from a Father Petru Paulet to teach in his parish nursery school in Câmpulung-Muscel in Romania and to help run the summer school for young people. Here the Sisters work with other volunteers. In 1996 in Câmpulung-Muscel a primary school has been started. This is ecumenical in that Orthodox children are taught with Catholic children and priests from both churches take religious education classes. Also in 1996, a new house has been opened for the ministry of families in need.

Subsequently, many more Sisters of St. Paul have become involved in this work and from it has evolved a Romanian novitiate for Sisters of St. Paul. There is much for them to do in the Lord's vineyard in Romania. At the end of 1996, the Archbishop of Bucharest and his priests were already asking for

the Sisters of St. Paul to carry their ministry to other towns. These missions are financed by the Sisters of St. Paul, Selly Park, with help from donations from supporters in the U.K. and Ireland. This is in keeping with the tradition of the Congregation, which itself could not have survived without financial support from the Sisters of St. Paul of Chartres 150 years ago.

Seemingly the Congregation produces an important new shoot every fifty years or so: England in 1847; Ireland in 1903; South Africa in 1954; and now Romania in the 1990s. Some of the older ministries have changed or ended. Child care in orphanages has ceased. Sisters are less involved in tertiary education

Below: Bucharest. 1991.
Nursery Class.

tertiary education and their participation in English secondary education has diminished. However, the commitment to primary education continues in four countries. Care of the elderly continues, as does parish work and catechetics. New ministries are emerging as the Congregation tries to remain faithful to its charism in responding to people's needs. So the Congregation looks forward to the next stage, confident that the future path will evolve keeping in mind the mission statement, adopted at the 1992 General Chapter expressing the charism which has been lived for one hundred and fifty years:

Rooted in Christ, we, religious women, inspired by St. Paul and our Foundress, Geneviève Dupuis, choose to stand with and for powerless people.

1 In Abergavenny in 1899. It was closed by Mother Foundress two years later.
2 For all the above, see Box 40 / 304
3 Box 44 / 328

Left: Câmpulung Muscel. Ceremony of Entrance to the Novitiate of first four Romanian Sisters of St. Paul.25.3.1995. Sister Maria Rosa Superior General with novices.

Right: The Cloister, Selly Park, Birmingham

The Voice of

'To appreciate the treasures of the Faith one must live in England. I have never really valued it. How much more difficult it must be for these poor Protestants, even those who have been well educated, to understand even the simplest truths of our holy religion. The whole thing to them is a puzzle or, as they say, "very funny." I weep for these wandering souls.'

- to the Bishop of Chartres, 9 February 1849

'I am now much engaged in putting our holy Rule into French and unfortunately some gnats have fed so copiously on my face and even in the corners of my eyes that I am nearly blind. Oh it burns so much and itches so much I could tear my eyes out. I after [sic, for 'offer'] up the pain I have.'

- to 'My dear Children in Christ' at Selly Park, Rome, 17 November 1863

'Do not cease to try to become better. It takes a long time to make a saint ... Give up that careless way of praying and going through your religious exercises.'

- to Sr Jane Berchman, Worcester, no date

'Do be careful about your chest. Don't cease to put on that chamois leather. It is as good as flannel. Write often to me.'

- to 'my dear child Joannes', 25 May 1885

'You are not an angel, my dear Child, you may expect to be tempted, but temptation is not sin. It gives you an occasion of merit if you resist. Try not to resent any words that prick your pride.'

- to an unknown Sister, 7 May 1887

'Dear me, what a little old nun you will soon be. 39!! on the 20th.'

- to Sr Presentation, 11 May

'The fish we have here from O'Brien is always very fresh, only 3d a lb., and he pays half the carriage ... I have written to tell him that you will most likely give him an order for Wednesday next.'

- addressee and date unknown

Extract from baptismal register - Geneviève Dupuis, 30th January 1813

55

Geneviève Dupuis

'I bless you as a loving mother blesses her loved and devoted child ... I embrace you and place you in the Sacred Heart.'

- to Sr M Xavier, 11 November 1897

'It came to mind that you ought sometimes to take Portwine *[sic]*. Mind, I will have you take care of your health. It is ours, not yours. Feed your poor donkey, else it lies down when you want to work.'

- addressee and date unknown

'I can't go on. I so very tired *[sic]* and overdone by the heat and so many people coming.'

- to Sr Mecthilde in Droitwich, 3 August 1894(?)

'How is your dear mother and your sister? How are the little ones? How old are they? Babies I suppose, five or six years old. My dear child, I pray for you daily. Be a good religious, recollected. Keep silence and see that it is kept by your Sisters. Obedience must be the virtue of the young religious.'

- addressee unknown, 23 September 1895

'... take the management, with Sr Guiseppa, of the senior school and leave the infant school to Sr St Benedict ... I should like you to teach [her] the Infant School System ... Give a treat to your Sisters and children at the convent from me ... Take care of that body [of yours] ... Continue your oils and take something between meals, if necessary. Let Sr Celine buy some good red flannel to make you some singlets. She will have to pay 2/4 or 2/6 a yard else it won't be good.'

- to Sr Xavier, 12 October 1897

'Therefore, my dear children. I do implore you, with a mother's love and anxiety, to set yourselves to cultivate above all things mutual charity, so that it be not only our profession, but the very instinct of us all to detect in ourselves every thought, word or deed which savours not of charity, and our practice humbly to correct.'

- to all her Sisters and Children, 15 January 1877

(Top): First approval of congregation the 'brief laudatif' from Pope Pius IX 5th March 1864
(Bottom): French passport Geneviève Dupuis, 1863

Superiors General

1847 - 1903
*Mother Geneviève Dupuis
(Sr. Zoile), Foundress*

1903 Jul. - Dec
Mother Gabriel Johnson

1904 - 1906
Mother. M. Benedicta Brodhurst

1906 - 1924
Mother Mecthilde Thelen

1924 - 1947
Mother Mary John of S.H. Barry

1947 - 1953
Mother M. Borgia Fitzgerald

1953 - 1968
Mother Cecilia Marie Auterson

1968 - 1980
Mother Malachy Joseph Lynch

1980 - 1986
Sister Sheila Mulcahy

1986 -
Sister Maria Rosa O'Sullivan

1847 - 1903

1903 Jul-Dec

1904 - 1906

1906 - 1924

1924 - 1947

1947 - 1953

1953 - 1968

1968 - 1980

1980 - 1986

1986 -

"*Sisters Reminisce*"

'*I always wanted to be a Sister. Under God, I owe my vocation to my wonderful parents...*'

'I was born in the shadow of one of our schools. I've known the Community since I was a little child until today, when I'm an old lady.'

'*There were 66 in the Novitiate when I entered in 1933: 36 postulants and 30 novices.*'

'We got up at 5.30, had two lectures a day (and elocution lessons) and did a lot of polishing, scrubbing, washing and starching ... You didn't say you wanted this or that, you took it.'

'*Mother Rose, the novice mistress, was a disciplinarian. Penances included eating breakfast on your knees.*'

'The strict silence was hard. You'd be bursting to say something, but couldn't - not until Recreation ... We communicated in lots of other ways.'

'*It was hard, but I was very happy. I didn't have any fear of anybody.*'

'Mother Ignatius, the novice mistress, was a very spiritual person.'

'Very few of us had nuns in the family - except maybe an aunt or great-aunt or a cousin.'

'We have several times had four, five, even six Sisters enter from the same family.'

'One sister was all set to join the Holy Faith nuns when a cousin who had been in prison in Wakefield came home saying, "Those Selly Park Sisters are the best nuns in the world. They used to come to visit us."

'One of the Sisters had met Mother Foundress when she was a little girl and been given a doll in a box by her. She venerated it. Mother Foundress loved flowers. She was very spiritual, mystical.'

'Mother Mary John Barry was very strict, but a wonderful person. She had to pull the order together after her predecessor's illness.'

'She had been in my life from the day she came to Kilfinane ... She finally got me in ... She had a great influence on us ... I bow my head instinctively at the Holy Name. If I didn't, I'd expect to get a tap on the back of

From left to right: 1. Entrance to Novitiate - Clothing Ceremony, 1966.
2. Novices in the kitchen, before 1966.
3. Musselburgh. Celebrating a Golden Jubilee in a branch House, 1948.
4. Golden Jubilarians, 1969.
5. Final Profession Ceremony. Superior General, Mother Cecilia Auterson and her First Assistant, Mother Marie de Sales placing the crowns Date probably 1953-1957?
6. Visit of Pope Paul II to Britain, 1982. Sisters with the Pope at Coventry.

That's why she joined.'

'My aunt, a Dominican nun, said, "I'll tell you of a great order in England which will suit you, the Selly Park nuns." That's how I came to join them'.

'I first made contact with the order when I came to St Gerard's Hospital to train as a nurse. The example of the Sisters made me decide to enter ...'

'My father always said that if the pope told him to take Epsom Salts he'd take them.'

my head from her. She's very much alive for me still ...'

'(Mother Cecilia) was a women of great vision. It took more courage to send Sisters to Africa than it had done to send them to Ireland in 1903.'

'Mother Borgia was very different: very simple, innocent. She'll have got a great welcome in Heaven.'

'We're very friendly. We don't have lots of rules and formality. We know one

another from our novitiate days. Before
we were allowed to go home on holidays,
we used to go to other houses for a rest
and change. That helped us to keep in
touch ...'
*'We didn't have a two-tier structure of choir
nuns and laysisters. There are no privileges.
We're all the same.'*
'We went out from Selly Park like
missioners, like the first disciples in small
groups.'
*'We worked in often poor and small schools,
parish schools. They didn't belong to us.
We lived in terraced houses among the poor,
not in big convents...'*
'But we used to spend so much time on
starching.'
*'We've always had time for people.
Whoever comes is welcome.'*
*'Perhaps we've not been too good at
preserving our records. We've been too*

*busy getting on with the job. And the Rule
warns us not to brag'.*

'The children we taught were very poor
but lovely and very bright.'
*'They were all Catholics. 80 per cent of
them were very good Catholics.'*
'Today's teachers can't know the
children as we did - they spend so much
time at meetings and filling forms.'
*'Some of the children we took out onto the
moors had never even seen a chicken.'*
'The classes were very big - 40 or 50'.
*'There were 300 children in the school ...
Today children have so much. Then they
had nothing.'*
'The penny Catechism gave then a
doctrine for life ... something they could
always fall back on.'
*'We didn't have so many broken homes then
... Many children haven't people they can*

trust today. We knew the children and their parents well ... Because we were Sisters parents trusted us. They knew we would take special care of their children.'

'We weren't just teachers. We hear a lot about "parish sisters" today. But we were parish sisters, and always have been. Every evening I used to go out visiting the children's homes, especially if there was any trouble, like a bereavement ... I went to every house. Some thought at first I was a nurse.'

'We visited the sick. We fed people at their doors and took in their washing. We made the children's dresses for their first Holy Communion and Confirmation and lots of clothing for the poor. That taught me the meaning of being a Sister of Charity.'

'We picked up coal on the shore and used to light people's fires. We used Sisters' salaries to buy food for the poor.'

'They wouldn't bury anyone until the Sisters had come round and said the Rosary.'

'As women we could say and do things that a priest couldn't. We were often go-betweens - between laypeople and clergy. They instinctively put their trust in us.'

'Father said, "I don't want you to be doing the flowers and cleaning the church. You're not going to be a sacristan. I want you to be a parish helper." I was like a curate.'

'We helped to put a lot of marriages right ... One woman said she'd been longing to be reconciled for years.'

'The wife said, "He'll insult you." He didn't, because there was a basket of kittens there and I played with them.'

'Many of them were good people who'd just drifted away, got married in a Registry Office ... or they'd been hurt by

Selly Park. 1972. Celebrating the 125th Anniversary Group Photograph outside "Bishop's Door" i.e. old mansion front door.

Profession of Vows

Lord Jesus Christ, in the Power of your Spirit, I desire to respond to Your call to labour with You for the greater glory of the Father, and the coming of His Kingdom, in honour of the Blessed Virgin Mary conceived without sin, and of Saint Paul the Apostle.

Therefore I, Sister... vow to God forever, Chastity for the Kingdom, Evangelical Poverty, and Religious Obedience, according to the Constitutions of the Sisters of Charity of St. Paul the Apostle.

Likewise, I promise of my own free will, in the presence of you, Sister... my Superior General, that with the help of God, I will faithfully observe these holy vows, as a Sister of Charity of Saint Paul the Apostle, and I bind myself to live according to the Constitutions of this Congregation.

Lord Jesus Christ, grant that, united with Your sacrifice of praise, I remain faithful.

something. People get hurt.'
'Miracles happened ... I knew she would be reconciled.'
'The husband grumbled about the new church that was being built. I said, "You could build a cathedral if you all did your bit." He was hardened, but his heart was soft. The Lord was just waiting for him.'
'You did everything in the parish - running sodalities, Children of Mary, summer schools, instructing converts, catechism classes.'
'It broke my heart to see children leaving school at 15 and wondering how they would face up to things ... But even if they strayed a little they came back. Now they don't. They're caught in a web.'

'Instead of building a new teacher-training college it was decided to acquire Newbold Revel. Sr Cecilia wanted students to benefit from being in a lovely building in beautiful surroundings. She felt very strongly about the importance of this. She herself led a very austere life, but she would say to us students during the holidays - "Tomorrow you must have a day out, a whole day. Take a picnic." She had a very broad, liberal view of education.'
'She was a real mother. She gave us space and freedom not usually given to young religious. She encouraged us as persons.'
'We were training teachers to work in schools - parish schools - as we had done.'

'I spent all my life at Coleshill looking after the children in St Edward's. I couldn't say how many young boys I've been a mother to.'
'They still come back to see me. They are doing well. One came back only yesterday - and he's retired! That tells you how old I must be.'
'We used to nurse them when they were sick and clothe them. Most of the boys went on to St Vincent's to learn a trade and out to work. I remember them all.'
'Seventeen Spanish children, including two senoritas, suddenly arrived in 1937 to escape the Spanish Civil War. I hadn't a word of Spanish but we managed to get on somehow. They were lively, beautiful.'
'Fr Hudson was very tall and stately, always the gentleman - and a great musician. He was ahead of his time.'
'The future Cardinal Griffin was wonderful with children. He played football with them. In the war he was an air-raid warden.'
'Sisters used to go over to Canada to see how our children were getting on.'
'Getting up at nights during the war to take the children into the shelters was dreadful.'
'Sr Benoit could tell off the boys without falling out with them.'

'A parish priest might be a bit awkward sometimes. But they were usually great ... I never felt exploited or trodden on.'
'Most priests would have been terrified lest Mother General withdrew the Sisters. They were proud of us and grateful.'

'A parish priest knew he could get rid of a Sister by having a quiet word with Mother General. But they can't do that with lay heads and teachers now!'

'The parish priest couldn't bring himself to tell the people that the Sisters were leaving and the school would close.'

'We did all we could to warn everyone and explain why the school would have to close because of the shortage of Sisters, though we would do all we possibly could to keep it open. Some parents said angrily "Why aren't there Sisters?" I answered, "Have you done anything to encourage your daughters to think about the religious life? Where do you think Sisters come from?"'

'The parents begged the priest: "Don't let the nuns go."'

'We have had to let go of many of our schools. That caused a lot of anxiety. Will their Catholic character be maintained? There are many loyal laypeople out there to take over, so we must trust in God.'

'Vatican II didn't knock us sideways. We were already used to living in small houses or flats, among the people and were very "open" to the world.'

'We had assumed that everything would continue to flourish and expand, and that life would go on more or less as it had always done. We assumed there would always be people behind us, following us, to carry on the work, as there had been hitherto.'

'Changes needed to happen.'

'If God wants us to have new postulants He will send them. If he wants new orders he'll start them.'

'In Romania there is real poverty and making do. That's Our Lord's way.'

'The Congregation will have a new lease of life.'

'I have been 66 years in the order ... I retired after 44 years of teaching - but then went on to do some more teaching, then to be a Sister in charge and finally went to a parish.'

'I was a headteacher for 35 years and after "retiring" was a superior of another house for ten years and then a parish sister.'

'I have spent 62 years at Coleshill.'

'I worked among the elderly for 22 years. I've had a very happy life.'

'I've had a busy life. I wouldn't change it for anything else.'

'I thought my career was over, but then I started an exciting new one.'

'After "retiring" I did almost twenty years working among the old, the poor and lonely. They were the best years of my life.'

'It's lovely at the end of life to come back to the mother house and have time to look at the sky and listen to the birds. Very fulfilling.'

Mother House and Branch Houses

Chronological order of opening   c = approximate date   Tr = transferred

Opened	Place	Name	Closed
1847	Banbury	St. John's Priory	Tr. 1990
1850	Brighton		1852
1850	West Bromwich		c 1853
1852	Leamington	St. Peters's	1984
1852	Marlow		1885
1853	Belmont	SS. Peter & Paul	1859
1853	Birmingham	St. Chad's	1966
1853	Burnley		1859
1853	Glossop	St. Paul's	1903
1853	Walsall	St. Patrick's	1862
1854	Birmingham	Erdington	1856
1854	Leeds	St. Patrick's	1990
1854	Radford	St. Mary's	1962

1856	Appleton	St. Bede's	c 1869
1856	Bath		?
1856	Ditton		1863
1856	Rainhill	St. Mary's	
1857	Bradford	St. Mary's	1865
1857	Lydiate		c 1869
1857	Macclesfield		?
1857	Spetchley		1863
1858	Wakefield	St. Joseph's	1957
1859	Bradford	St. Patrick's	1989
1859	Brewood	St. Mary's	c 1862
1859	Garstang	St. Michael's	1968
1859	Holywell/Imger Gerddi	St. Winefride's/Gerddi Beuno	
1859	Kendal	St. Mary's	1968
1859	Leeds	St. Anne's	1895
1859	Prescot		c 1863
1859	Southport	St. Marie's	
1860	Crosby	SS. Peter & Paul	1960
1860	Hurst Green	St. Joseph's	c 1872
1861	Dudley	St. Anne's	1987
1861	Gillmoss	St. Swithin's	c 1863
1861	Hadfield	St. Joseph's	1976
1861	Neston		c 1861
1861	Selby	St. Mary's	c 1876
1862	Crook	St. Mary's	1910
1862	Marton	St. Ann's	c 1870
1862	Middlesbrough		c 1867
1864	Birmingham	St. Paul's, Selly Park	
1864	Brownedge	St. Benedict's	1969
1865	Danesfield	St. Charles	1885
1868	Birmingham	Nechells, St. Joseph's	1953
1868	Thorndon	Our Lady's	1901

1869	Blackhill	St. Mary's	
1870	Chipping Campden	St. Paul's	
1870	Holywell	Hospice	
1870	Liverpool	Woolton	1891
1870	Whitehaven	St. Anne's	1996
1871	Costessey	St. Augustine's	1976
1872	Stockton-on-Tees	St. Mary's	1987
1872	Stourbridge	St. Joseph's	
1873	Atherstone		c 1876
1873	Birmingham	Smethwick, St. Philip's	?
1873	Maryport	St. Paul's	c 1964
1874	Avon Dassett	St. Joseph's	1910
1874	Worcester	St. George's	1984
1874	York	St. Wilfrid's	1994
1876	Batley	St. Mary's	1991
1876	Glossop	St. Mary's	
1876	Workington	St. Michael's	
1878	Cleator Moor	St. Mary's	1887
1878	Everingham	St. Everilda's	1892
1878	Shipley		c 1879
1879	Cheltenham	St. Gregory's	1935
1879	Seaham Harbour	St. Francis of Sales	1886
1880	Birnie Knowe		1882
1880	Brooms	St. Joseph's	1974
1880	Goole		c 1880
1880	Whitwick	Holy Cross	1888
1881	Newcastle	St. Andrew's	1942
1881	Studley	St. Mary's	Tr. 1960
1882	Birmingham	St. Michael's	?

1883	Darlington	St. William's	1982
1884	Coleshill	St. Paul's	1930
1884	Teddington	St. Paul's	
1885	Exton	St. Francis of Assisi	1918
1886	Birmingham	St. Vincent's	1935
1886	Boston	St. Mary's	1978
1887	Llanarth		1903
1887	Ripon	St. Wilfrid's	1989
1888	Kidderminster	St. Ambrose	1978
1889	Birmingham	St. Catherine's	1904
1889	Esh Laude	St. Michael's	1979
1890	Oswestry	Our Lady & St. Oswald	
1891	Hounslow	St. Joseph's	
1892	Bradford	St. Cuthbert's, Manningham	1921
1899	Abergavenny	St. Michael's	1901
1903	Bradford	St. Joseph's, Manningham	1905
1903	Kilfinane	St. Paul's	
1903	Oakamoor	St. Teresa's	1955
1904	Axminster	St. Paul's	1910
1904	Selby	St. Mary's	1954
1905	Keyham	St. Martha's	
1905	Lanchester	All Saints'	1957
1906	Coleshill	St. Edward's	
1907	Billinge	Our Lady's	Tr. 1962
1907	Galashiels	The Convent	1927
1907	Musselburgh	St. Anne's	
1907	Ottawa	St. George's Home	1935

1908	Birmingham	St. Paul's, Vernon Road	
1908	Dipton	The Convent	1978
1908	Liverpool	Great Mersey St., St. Joseph's	1922
1908	Stanley	St. Joseph's	1910
1913	Coleshill	St. Gerard's	1993
1916	Besford Court		Tr. 1924
1919	Shefford	St. Francis	1944
1919	Taunton		1920
1920	Birmingham	Beechenhurst	1939
1922	Birstall	St. Joseph's	
1923	Birmingham	Handsworth, St. Augustine's	1956
1923	Sutton Manor	St. Teresa's	1980
1924	Penketh	St. Joseph's	1927
1924	Sambourne	St. Joseph's	Tr. 1950
1925	Bradford	St. William's, Girlington	1987
1925	Sutton Coldfield	St. Paul's	
1926	Leeds	St. Augustine's	1974
1926	Sunbury	St. Teresa's	1988
1927	Buckfast	St. Mary's	1987
1927	Kilmallock	St. Joseph's / St. Pauls's	
1927	Walsall	St. Patrick's	1978
1928	Standish	St. Teresa's	1963
1930	Formby	St. Paul's	1972
1930	Wednesbury	St. Mary's	1959
1930	Wimborne	St. Cuthberga's	1971
1931	Coleshill	St. Joan's	1989
1931	Parkstone	St. Paul's	1994

1932	Longton	St. Gregory's	
1933	Heaton Mersey	St. Winifred's	
1934	Dublin	Blackrock College	1995
1934	Penketh, Great Sankey	St. Joseph's	Tr. 1965
1935	Ashton in Makerfield	St. Joseph's	1974
1935	Wakefield, Lupset	Our Lady of Good Counsel	1984
1939	Woodchester	St. Paul's College	Tr. 1946
1941	Birmingham	Archbishop's House	
1942	Newcastle, Denton Burn	St. Bede's	1993
1943	Birmingham	Woodville	1973
1944	Westminster	Archbishop's House	1957
1946	Newbold Revel	St. Paul's College	1978
1948	Cheadle	St. Joseph's	1961
1950	Croome Court	St. Joseph's	Tr. 1979
1950	Grange over Sands	Our Lady's	1970
1951	Birmingham	Northfield, St. Brigid's	
1951	Loftus	St. Paul's	1970
1953	Birmingham	Annie Bright Weston House	
1954	Birmingham	Great Barr, Holy Name	1965
1954	Langley	St. Paul's	
1954	Modimong	St. Anne's	1993
1954	Zeerust	St. Mary's	1970
1955	Leicester	Evington Hall	1992
1956	Clonakilty	St. Paul's, Bushmount	
1957	Bradford	Heaton Mount	1967

1958	Dawlish	St. Paul's, The Rise	
1959	Coventry	Corpus Christi	
1959	Coventry	St. Paul's	1990
1962	Aston Hall	Aston Hall	
1962	Wavertree	Our Lady's	1982
1963	Rustenburg	Selly Park, Convent	
1964	Birmingham	Cathedral House	1984
1964	Dublin	St. Paul's, Greenhills	
1965	Penketh, Larch Ave.	St. Joseph's	1996
1966	Hammanskraal	St. Peter's Seminary	1976
1970	Birmingham	University Chaplaincy	1990
1970	Shrewsbury	Bishop's Household	
1976	Leeds	Headingley	1984
1976	Minsteracres		
1977	Pretoria	Archbishop's House	1989
1977	Southport	St. Patrick's	
1978	Coventry	Holy Family	
1978	Coventry	St. Mary's	1988
1978	Heronbrook, Knowle	Heronbrook House	
1978	Princethorpe	Princethorpe College	1987
1979	Besford Court	St. Joseph's	1996
1979	Birmingham	Olton	1983
1979	Limerick	Bishop's House	1995
1980	Birmingham	Harborne	1993
1980	Birmingham	Maryvale Centre	
1980	Phokeng		1990
1981	Birmingham	West Indian Chaplaincy	
1981	Liverpool	Archbishop's House	1996
1981	South Shields		1989

1982	Warrington	Sacred Heart	
1983	Hawkestone Hall		1988
1986	Burn Hall	St. Joseph's House of Prayer	1992
1986	Oldbury	George Simmons House	1993
1988	Birmingham	Billesley	
1988	Birmingham	Highgate	
1988	Cape Town	St. Paul's	
1988	Glasgow	St. Peter's	1993
1988	Maidenhead	St. Paul's	
1988	Solihull	Maranatha / St. Brigid's	
1990	Banbury	St. Genevieve's	
1990	Birmingham	Handsworth, St. Paul's	
1990	Leeds	Moor Drive	
1990	Wakefield	St. Paul's	1995
1991	Birmingham	Handsworth, St. Joseph's	
1991	Bucharest, Romania	Strada Rosmarin	1992
1991	Mogwase	Bethany	
1992	Bucharest, Romania	Bulevardul Unirii	
1992	Bucharest, Romania	Floreasca	1994
1992	Bucharest, Romania	Piata Concordiei	1994
1992	Mogwase	Holy Family	1996
1994	Câmpulung Muscel, Romania	Parohia R.C.	
1994	Church Ernstone	Lynton Cottage	
1994	Hackney	St. Paul's	
1995	Câmpulung Muscel, Romania	Novitiate	
1995	Teddington	248, Kingston Rd.	
1996	Câmpulung Muscel, Romania	Casa Ieremia Valahul	
1996	Warrington, Westbrook	St. Joseph's	
1997	Motru, Romania		
1997	Tirgoviste, Romania		

Sisters of Charity of St. Paul the Apostle
Alphabetical List of Houses

Abergavenny

Key:
Place
House
Diocese, Dates
Ministry
Requested by, or patron
General information

Abergavenny
St. Michael's
Cardiff, 1899- 1901
Parish school / parish visiting
Probably requested by bishop
Mrs. Herbert of Llanover was involved
with the provision of the house.

Appleton
St. Bede's
Liverpool, 1856-c1869
Parish schools
Bishop Alexander Goss of Liverpool

Ashton in Makerfield
St. Joseph's
Liverpool, 1935- 1974
Parish schools / parish visiting
Request from Parish Priest,
Father O' Meara
Sisters travelled initially from Billinge and
from Rainhill, 1974 until 1983.

Aston Hall
Aston Hall
Birmingham, 1962-
Care of elderly diocesan priests
Requested by Archbishop Grimshaw

of Birmingham
Mr. C.S. Hartley bought and presented
house to the diocese for retired priests. It
was once a Passionist House, home of
Blessed Dominic Barberi.

Atherstone
Birmingham, c1873-c1876
Parish school

Avon Dassett
St. Joseph's
Birmingham, 1874- 1910
*Catholic school / parish visiting / small
orphanage / boarding school*
Mr. and Mrs. Perry of Bitham House
gave cottage for Sisters
Scholars were few, so orphans taken as
well. Sisters were to "cultivate a Catholic
Spirit in the village." Mr. and Mrs. Perry
also built the church and the school.

Axminster
St. Paul's
Plymouth, 1904- 1910
Parish school
Probably Bishop Charles Graham of
Plymouth and Mr. William Knight
Probably Rev. Mother Gabriel Johnson's
foundation, although opened after her
death. Closed because there were "too
few Catholics and little scope for work."

Banbury
St. John's Priory
Birmingham, 1847-

Parish schools / private and night
schools / parish visiting
Dr. Tandy requested Sisters from
Sisters of St. Paul of Chartres
Sisters first lived in presbytery. St. John's
Priory bought in 1851 becoming Mother
House and Novitiate until the transfer to
Selly Park, 1864. Sisters travelled to
school in Brailes 1935 - 1939. 1990
convent closed, private school leased.
Sisters left St. John's School, transferred to
St. Genevieve's Convent, Edmunds Road
and work in St. Joseph's School and
parish.

Bath
Clifton, c1856- ?

Batley
St. Mary's
Leeds, 1876-1991
Parish schools / parish visiting
Invited by Bishop Gordon, former
Parish Priest
Sisters travelled to Birstall until 1922.

Belmont
S.S. Peter & Paul
Cardiff, 1853- 1859
Parish school
Perhaps Fathers Berry and Broderick.
In 1853 Father Lambe came.
Small chapel opened 2.2.1853. On
26.7.1853 First Mass said in school-chapel
of SS. Peter & Paul "quickly built together
with a tiny convent ."

Besford Court
St. Joseph's
Birmingham, 1916- 1996
*Residential education and care of boys
with special needs*
Archdiocese of Birmingham
Junior boys with Sisters transferred to
Sambourne 1924, Croome Court 1950,
returned to Besford 1979 and girls
included.

Billinge
Our Lady's
Liverpool, 1907- 1982
Residential child care and parish school
Father Berry of Liverpool Diocesan
Rescue Society
Sisters took over Greenfield House and
school. In 1962 the home was transferred
to Wavertree. It was closed in 1982.

Birmingham
Annie Bright Weston House
Birmingham, 1953-
Care of the elderly
Archdiocese of Birmingham
Mr. Weston gave house on Wake Green
Rd. to Archdiocese after the death of his
wife, who was Bishop Bright's sister. 1966
moved to 6, Norfolk Rd. Later leased by
the Congregation.

Birmingham
Archbishop's House
Birmingham, 1941-
*Archbishop's household: domestic
management*
Archbishop Williams of Birmingham
First at 6, Norfolk Rd., then Barnt Green
and 8, Shadwell St. Archbishops
Masterson, Grimshaw, Dwyer and Couve
de Murville followed Archbishop
Williams.

Birmingham
Beechenhurst
Birmingham, 1920-1939
*Residence for secular students in Selly
Park Training College*
Congregation
1939 College evacuated to Woodchester
and Beechenhurst sold.

Birmingham
Billesley, Bethany House
Birmingham, 1988-
Parish work
Parish Priest

Birmingham
Cathedral House
Birmingham, 1964- 1984
*Domestic management of Cathedral
clergy household / sacristy*
Archdiocese of Birmingham
Sisters left in 1984, because of shortage of
personnel caused by ageing and ill health.

Birmingham
Erdington
Birmingham, 1854- 1856
Parish school

Birmingham
Great Barr, Holy Name
Birmingham, 1954- 1965
*Parish schools / catechetics: converts
and children from non-RC schls..*
AMDG School - Parish funded. Sisters
unsalaried until 1954, when new school
built. Sisters travelled from St. Chad's
1940 -1954. Convent in Walsall Rd., 1954
and in Newtown Rd., 1959. Sisters
travelled to St. Augustine's, Handsworth
from 1958.

Birmingham
Handsworth, St. Augustine's
Birmingham, 1923-
*Parish school / parish visiting
counselling (from 1991)*
Parish Priest
House closed in 1958 (road scheme).
Sisters travelled from Vernon Rd., three
houses in Great Barr & St. Chad's until
1965. Sisters returned to parish, St.
Joseph's Convent in 1991.

Birmingham
Handsworth, St. Paul's
Birmingham, 1990-
Novitiate and open community
Congregation

Birmingham
Harborne
Birmingham, 1980- 1993
*Care of the elderly in sheltered
accommodation.*

Birmingham
Highgate
Birmingham, 1988-
Parish schools / The Fireside Centre

Birmingham
Maryvale Centre
Birmingham, 1980-
*Diocesan Pastoral and Educational
Centre*
Archdiocese of Birmingham

Birmingham
Nechells St. Joseph's
Birmingham, 1868- 1953
Parish school / parish visiting
Convent closed in 1953 and Sisters
travelled from St. Chad's until 1966.

Birmingham

Birmingham
Northfield, St. Brigid's
Birmingham, 1951-
Parish primary school / parish visiting catechetics for other pupils
Sisters travelled from Selly Park until convent opened at 24, Woodland Rd. Then Frankley Beeches Rd. Began with 280 pupils from 26 schools, further 200 at evening catechetics classes.

Birmingham
Olton
Birmingham, 1979- 1983
Care of the elderly in sheltered accommodation

Birmingham
St. Paul's, Selly Park
Birmingham, 1864-
Mother House / Infirmary / Novitiate until 1990 / St. Edward's parish school feeding poor / Overseas student Sisters other schools / Hospice / Retreat and Conference Centre / Fireside Centre
Bishop Ullathorne
Sisters moved from Banbury 1864. Original House built 1830's. Nineteenth Century extensions, Church 1914-1916, New Infirmary 1934. Generalate. Mother House, i.e. home for all Sisters. All other houses are branch houses from Selly Park.

Birmingham
Smethwick, St. Philip's
Birmingham, c1873-c1880
Parish school

Birmingham
St. Catherine's
Birmingham, 1889- 1904
Parish schools / parish visiting
Canon Fenn, p.p., friend of Mother Foundress. He died 1891.

Birmingham
St. Chad's
Birmingham, 1853-1966
Parish schools / parish visiting catechetics / teacher training
Followed Sisters of Mercy
First at Bath St. 1865 moved to 16, Whittall St. - Centre for pupil teacher training and adult night classes. Also served St. John's, St. Michael's, St. Peter's Schools. House of Studies until 1934. After 1966, until 1982 Sisters travelled to school from St. Paul's, Vernon Rd.

Birmingham
St. Michael's
Birmingham, 1882- ?
Parish schools
Served St. John's School from 1882 (Previously served from St. Chad's)

Birmingham
St. Paul's College
Birmingham, 1910- 1978
Teacher Training (non resident until Beechenhurst bought)
Congregation
Previously Sisters trained at Banbury and Whittall St. In 1910 twelve Sisters started training at Selly Park.(St. Brigid's and St. Martha's wing). 1914 new block (Later Novitiate) built for forty students. Grant given 1927. Transferred to Woodchester 1939 and Newbold Revel 1946. Later, degree courses offered, men and women students.

Birmingham
St. Paul's, Vernon Rd
Birmingham, 1908-
Secondary school for RC Girls Preparatory (private) school / House of Studies (Sisters at University)

Bishop Ilsley requested Congregation to finance and build school.
First at 16 & 18, Vernon Rd. 1939 new convent and preparatory school built. From 1976 - new buildings. Became Grammar, then Comprehensive School.

Birmingham
St. Vincent's
Birmingham, 1886- 1953
Parish school / parish visiting
First in Ashted Row. 1931 new school built and convent moved to Great Brook St. Sisters travelled to school from St. Chad's 1953 - 1966.

Birmingham
University Chaplaincy
Birmingham, 1970- 1990
Chaplaincy to students.

Birmingham
West Indian Chaplaincy
Birmingham, 1981-
Chaplaincy to West Indian Community in Birmingham
Diocesan request
Mission began 1974, when sisters travelled.

Birmingham
Woodville
Birmingham, 1943- 1973
Mother and Baby Home
Part of Father Hudson's Homes, Diocesan Rescue Society
Sisters took over from Catholic Women's League.

Birnie Knowe
Galloway, 1880-1882
Parish school
Also called Auchinlech and Old Cumnock. Mining community.

Birstall
St. Joseph's
Leeds, 1922-
Parish school / parish visiting
Father Lea, p.p. of Batley. Father Russell, new p.p. in Birstall (1906) 1877 school opened. 1881 sisters came. Lay staff 1894 - 1902 when Sisters returned. From 1881 they travelled from Batley until p.p. requested convent.

Blackhill
St. Mary's
Hexham & Newcastle, 1869-
Parish day and night schools / parish visiting / sodalities / instructing converts / sacristy work
School built 1859. Town of iron and steel works.

Blackrock College
Dublin, Ireland, 1934- 1995
New ministry in Boys' College: nursing, housekeeping, infirmary, linen room, dormitories, kitchen supervision
Holy Ghost Fathers, especially Rev. McQuaid, CSSp.
Later a Sister taught in Junior School and continues after 1995, living in Greenhills.

Boston
St. Mary's
Nottingham, 1886- 1978
Parish school / parish visiting
Miss Frances Smith, teacher, built convent and invited the Sisters

Bradford
St. William's, Girlington
Leeds, 1925- 1987
Parish primary and secondary schools parish visiting
From 1888 Sisters travelled from St.

Patrick's. New house, St. William's, built 1925. Sisters withdrew from Primary School in 1973, continued in Blessed Edmund Campion School until 1987.

Bradford
Heaton Mount
Leeds, 1957- 1967
Private school
Sisters and children moved from St. Patrick's Private School. New school was officially opened 1957 and closed in 1967 because of lack of numbers.

Bradford
St. Joseph's, Manningham
Leeds, 1903- 1905
Private school
Small school at Eldon Place. Bishop requested it to be expanded as Grammar School for girls. Congregation not able to do this, so it was handed over to Cross and Passion Sisters.

Bradford
St. Cuthbert's, Manningham
Leeds, 1892-1921
Parish school / parish visiting
Canon Earnshaw,p.p.
Convent in Victor St. was rented. Sisters went from St. Patrick's to new school for 200 pupils and withdrew because of "much sickness and scarcity of sisters elsewhere."

Bradford
St. Mary's
Leeds, 1857- 1865
Parish schools / parish visiting
Canon Harrison, p.p., requested sisters in 1854.
Sisters ran Sunday school and Parish school - 170 infants and girls in one room

When headteacher died, no certificated Sister available, so Sisters of Mercy came. Convent in Park Place.

Bradford
St. Patrick's
Leeds, 1859- 1989
Parish schools / parish visiting
Canon Harrison, p.p.
Schools for girls and infants began in 1859. Sisters came from St. Mary's. Much subsequent school reorganisation. Sisters went from here to St. William's.

Brewood
St. Mary's
Birmingham, c1859-c1862
Parish school
Probably closed when Sister - headteacher died.

Brighton
St. John the Baptist parish
Arundel & Brighton, 1850- 1852
Parish school
Bishop Grant or p.p.
Sisters unsalaried and all in their twenties. After some problem Mother Foundress withdrew, despite pleas from bishop and parish to stay.

Brooms
St. Joseph's
Hexham & Newcastle, 1880- 1974
Parish schools
Bishop Wilkinson
School opened with 400 pupils, mainly from mining village of Leadgate. A Pupil teachers' training scheme established. 1892 secondary education introduced

Brooms

Brownedge
St. Benedict's
Salford, 1864- 1969
Initially poor relief, especially of girls (no work in cotton mills) / parish school parish visiting
Father Walker, p.p. and Bishop William Turner of Salford
It was the last convent to be founded from Banbury and closed because of shortage of sisters.

Bucharest
Bulevardul Unirii
Bucharest, Romania, 1990
AIDS babies / street children / nursery schools / catechetics / English lessons for adults
Sisters volunteered for babies. Bishop and p.p. requested for schools.
Sisters lived at Colentina Hospital (1990-1), Strada Rosmarin (1991-2), Bulevardul Unirii (1992-); also in Piata Concordiei (Caritas Vienna) and Floreasca.

Buckfast
St. Mary's
Plymouth, 1927-1987
Parish school / parish visiting / sewing for Abbey
Benedictine monks of Buckfast Abbey
Convent belonged to Abbey. Sisters withdrew when schools re-organised

Burn Hall
St. Joseph's House of Prayer
Hexham & Newcastle, 1986- 1992
Liturgy and domestic responsibilities in House of Prayer
Requested by Father Josef Pichler MHM

Burnley
Salford, 1853- 1859
Parish school
Parish Priest
The Parish Priest demanded that the Sisters be independent of the Mother House. When Mother Foundress refused, he dismissed them. He later asked for their return but none were available.

Câmpulung Muscel
Casa Ieremia Valahul
Bucharest, Romania, 1996-
Ministry to the needy.

Câmpulung Muscel
Novitiate
Bucharest, Romania, 1995-
Formation House for Romanian Sisters of St. Paul

Câmpulung Muscel
Parohia Romano Catholica
Bucharest, Romania, 1994-
Parish schools / Summer school / SVP parish work
Father Paulet, Petru, p.p.
Sisters and staff from Vernon Road and other volunteers run the Summer School. House for candidates and postulants; also novices before Novitiate built.

Cape Town
St. Paul's
Cape Town, South Africa, 1988-
Training of Diocesan Catechetical Teams and preparing resources
Bishop Naidoo of Cape Town

Cheadle
St. Joseph's
Birmingham, 1948- 1962
Parish school / parish visiting

Sisters replaced Sisters of Penance of St. Dominic Later Sisters taught in Oakamoor. Sisters of Visitation from Bridport replaced Sisters of St. Paul.

Cheltenham
St. Gregory's
Clifton, 1879- 1935
Parish school / parish visiting
Benedictine p.p. Later a house was built by the Bingham family
Sisters left when a headmaster was appointed. Statues of Sacred Heart (in cloister) and Our Lady (outside chapel) in Selly Park given by Mrs. Bingham, who left money, which built Selly Park laundry.

Chipping Campden
St. Paul's
Clifton, 1870-
Parish school / parish visiting
Gainsborough family built church and school

Church Enstone
Lynton Cottage
Birmingham, 1994-
House for rest and recuperation for Sisters
Near to Radford and old Heythrop College.

Cleator Moor
St. Mary's
Lancaster, 1878- 1887
Parish school / parish visiting
Bishop Wilkinson
Convent in Trumpet St.

Clonakilty
St. Paul's, Bushmount
Cork & Ross, Ireland, 1956-

Nursing Home
Bishop Moynihan's request for a
home for retired and invalid priests

Coleshill
St. Edward's
Birmingham, 1906-
Home for boys / parish primary school
Father Hudson
Sisters came with boys when St. Paul's
Home closed. St. Edward's was the first of
the newly built homes in Coleshill. Home
closed in 1981. Convent continues.

Coleshill
St. Gerard's
Birmingham, 1913- 1993
*Orthopaedic Hospital / School of
Nursing and Physiotherapy*
Father Hudson
Began as an infirmary for sick boys. Also a
school on the wards and a Domestic
Science School, local clinics and mission
on the hopfields 1936-1947. Convent, St.
Philomena's, closed 1993. A Sister
continues to work in the Hospital.

Coleshill
St. Joan's
Birmingham, 1931- 1989
Child Care: Home for girls, initially
Father Hudson
First home for girls on the Coleshill site.
Later family groups and St. Teresa's
Nursery were established.

Coleshill
St. Paul's
Birmingham, 1884- 1930
*Child Care and Poor Law school for
boys*
Bishop Ullathorne
Boys and sisters moved to St. Edward's.

Home closed in 1930 - Government
reorganisation.

Costessey
St. Augustine's
East Anglia, 1871-1976
Parish schools / parish visiting
Jerningham family built school. Lord
and Lady Stafford asked for Sisters
Sisters withdrawn 1873 and returned
1877.

Coventry
Corpus Christi
Birmingham, 1959-
Parish schools / parish visiting
Parish Priest's request

Coventry
Holy Family
Birmingham, 1978-
*St. Paul's College Office (after closure)
parish work*

Coventry
St. Mary's
Birmingham, 1978- 1988
Parish work
Father Thornton, p.p.
A Sister continued from St. Paul's,
Coventry, 1988-9.

Coventry
St. Paul's
Birmingham, 1959- 1990
*Diocesan secondary schools / parish
visiting / catechetics*
Archdiocese
Convents in Longfellow Rd (1959), Orion
Crescent (1960), Potters Green Rd
(1962). Cardinal Wiseman Girls' Schools:
Secondary Modern, Grammar,
Comprehensive (finally mixed and lay

head). Catechetics in parishes of school
catchment area.

Crook
St. Mary's
Hexham & Newcastle, 1862- 1910
Parish schools / parish visiting
Father Wilkinson, p.p., Later Bishop
of Hexham and Newcastle
P.P.'s sister, Anglican nun who became
RC, told him of Sisters of St Paul.

Crosby
SS. Peter & Paul
Liverpool, 1860- 1960
Parish school / parish visiting
Bishop Alexander Goss of Liverpool
and Father Fisher,p.p.
Closed 1960 after death of Sister -
headteacher. Catholic teachers available
locally.

Danesfield
St. Charles
Northampton, 1865- 1885
Parish school
Probably Charles Robert Scott-
Murray

Darlington
St. William's
Hexham & Newcastle, 1883-1982
Parish schools / parish visiting
Bishop Wilkinson
Sisters followed Sisters of Mercy. Convent
in two terraced houses opposite church.
1952 new convent in Nestfield St.

Dawlish
St. Paul's, The Rise
Plymouth, 1958-
*Care of the elderly / guest house
(including house for Sisters).*

Dawlish

House had belonged to Congregation of the Nativity of Blessed Virgin Mary which amalgamated with Sisters of Charity of St. Paul in 1955.

Dipton
The Convent
Hexham & Newcastle, 1908- 1978
Parish schools / parish visiting
Closed because of shortage of sisters.

Ditton
Liverpool, 1856- 1863
Parish school
Bishop Alexander Goss of Liverpool

Dublin
St. Paul's, Greenhills
Dublin, Ireland, 1964-
Parish primary school / secondary school / parish work
Archbishop of Dublin
First convent in Wellington Lane.

Dudley
St. Anne's
Birmingham, 1861- 1987
Parish school, including "half timers" (factory children) / parish visiting
Father James Bond, p.p..
George Spencer, later Fr. Ignatius Spencer set up first Mass Centre. In 1987 compulsory purchase of convent (Road Scheme) and Sisters travelled from Stourbridge to school and hospital. A Sister travelled to Brierley Hill School from 1982 to 1987.

Esh Laude
St. Michael's
Hexham & Newcastle, 1889- 1979
Parish school / parish visiting
Bishop Wilkinson

Replaced by Sisters of Mercy from Alnwick. Near Ushaw. Church built in 1779 to look like a farm.

Everingham
St. Everilda's
Middlesbrough, 1878- 1892
Parish school
Lord Herries of Everingham Park
Sisters replaced another Community and were dismissed by Lord Herries without sanction of Bishop of Middlesbrough.

Exton
St. Francis of Assisi
Nottingham, 1885-1918
Parish schools / Parish visiting
Gainsborough family, probably
House closed 1918 because " it was impossible to replace certificated sisters and the place had many disadvantages."

Formby
St. Paul's
Liverpool, 1930- 1972
Parish school / parish visiting
Sisters travelled from Great Crosby from 1924 until new convent built 1930. Sisters withdrew in 1972 because of shortage of Sisters and were replaced by La Sagesse Sisters.

Galashiels
The Convent
Edinburgh, 1907-1927
Parish all age schools / parish visiting sacristy
Probably Canon Rooney, p.p.
Venerable Margaret Sinclair once a pupil here. Sisters left because of school reorganisation.

Garstang
St. Michael's
Lancaster, 1859- 1968
Parish school / parish visiting
Bishop Alexander Goss of Liverpool
Closed because no Sister available for replacement.

Gillmoss
St. Swithin's
Liverpool, c1861-c1863
Parish school

Glasgow
St. Peter's
Glasgow, 1988- 1993
Diocesan Pastoral Centre
Diocese
Joint ministry

Glossop
St. Mary's
Nottingham, 1876-
Parish schools / parish visiting
Parish Priest
Also called Howardtown. First convent in St. Mary's Rd. Later moved to Shaw St. and then to Sunlaws St. From 1968 a Sister in new School, St. Margaret's, in Gamesley.

Glossop
St. Paul's
Nottingham, 1853- 1903
Parish schools / parish visiting
Father Theodore Fauvel, French émigré priest.
Also called Old Glossop. School - All Saints. Sisters taught in St. Mary's from here at first.

Goole
Leeds, c1880-c1880
Parish school

Grange over Sands
Our Lady's
Lancaster, 1950- 1970
House for Sisters' rest and recuperation parish work

Hackney
St. Paul's
Westminster, 1994-
Programmes for people with HIV and AIDS / Catechetics / parish work
Ministry at first in Mildmay Mission Hospital.

Hadfield
St. Joseph's
Nottingham, 1861-1976
Parish school / parish visiting / parish work
Father Theodore Fauvel, p.p. Lord Howard gave cottage in Spring Gardens
First cottage - one room down, two up. New house in Hadfield Rd. built by John Dalton, related to Sister St. Louis Fisher.

Hammanskraal
St. Peter's Seminary
Pretoria, South Africa, 1965- 1976
Teaching and domestic organisation in seminaries
Diocese
Major and Minor Seminaries and conference centre.

Hawkstone Hall
Shrewsbury, 1983- 1988
Redemptorist Pastoral Centre
Redemptorists

Joint ministry.

Heaton Mersey
St. Winifred's
Salford, 1933-
Parish school / parish visiting / Private school / House of Studies
Parish Priest
Private School and House of Studies finished and House sold 1963, new convent bought. Sisters continue in parish work after retirement from school,1993.

Heronbrook, Knowle
Heronbrook House
Birmingham, 1978-
Therapeutic Centre for Priests and Religious
1996 initial ministry finished. New programmes developing. Also Maranatha, now St. Brigid's House, Solihull opened 1988.

Holywell
Hospice
Wrexham, 1870-
Hospice for Pilgrims
Parish Priest
Served from St. Winefride's Convent until 1970.

Holywell
St. Winefride's
Wrexham, 1959-
Parish school / private school / parish visiting
Father Lambert, S.J. (Rector of St. Beuno's). Miss Parry built house.
First Sisters lived in small cottage in Well St. 1870 moved to larger house, now demolished. 1970 Sisters withdrew from Primary School, moved to a new house -

Gerddi Beuno in Whitford St. on site of new Private school which closed 1984. Jesuits kept Star Inn, in penal times, and ministered to N Wales Catholics.

Hounslow
St. Joseph's
Westminster, 1891-
Parish school / parish visiting
Miss Beckwith of Bath Rd. donated land for church and school
Evidence of opposition from Protestant Alliance in early years. Hounslow was an important centre for stage coaches, now close to Heathrow Airport. Town and school multi-racial.

Hurst Green
St. Joseph's
Salford, c1860-c1872
Parish school
Bishop William Turner, Salford near Stoneyhurst.

Kendal
St.Paul's
Lancaster, 1859-1968
Parish school / parish visiting
Before Sisters came Catholics kept together by organist, Mr Wray, whose daughter, Susannah (Sister Camilla) entered in 1860. Closed because no Sisters to replace retiring headteacher. First convent in Hexham and Newcastle Diocese. Benedictine priests.

Keyham
St. Martha's
Plymouth, 1905-
Parish primary schools: Keyham Barton, Devonport / parish visiting
First Sisters in two houses next to Church. Keyham: initially no school

furniture or grant from Local Authority. Last Sister retired 1996, not replaced. Sister in Devonport School from 1985- Near to naval dockyard.

Kidderminster
St. Ambrose
Birmingham, 1888- 1978
Parish school / parish visiting / care for girls working in factories
Replaced Loreto Sisters. Sisters travelled from Stourbridge 1978 - 1988.

Kilfinane
St. Paul's
Limerick, Ireland, 1903-
Parish primary school / secondary school / parish visiting
Parish Priest
First branch house in Ireland. 1908 -new school after fire, 1987- new Scoil Pól.

Kilmallock
St. Joseph's
Limerick, Ireland, 1927-
Parish primary school / secondary school / parish visiting
Canon Begley,p.p.
First convent in Sarsfield St. New convent 1933, Irish Novitiate House during war 1939-1945. Present new convent, St. Paul's, in Glenfield Rd.

Lanchester
All Saints'
Hexham & Newcastle, 1905- 1957
Parish schools / parish visiting

Langley
St. Paul's
Salford, 1954-
Parish school / parish visiting
Parish Priest

A new parish for a new housing development. Sisters lived first in Seascale Walk, then in new convent in Wood St.

Leamington
St. Peter's
Birmingham, 1852- 1984
Parish schools / parish visiting / care of refugees 1914 - 1918
Mrs. Bishop gave house in Augusta Place and salaries
1913 Mr. Charles Shaw gave house in Milverton Terrace. Mrs. Bishop wanted to control Sisters. Mother Foundress refused, despite opposition from Père Sureau, Bishop Ullathorne, Dr. Tandy. Traditionally regarded as first branch house (Brighton shortlived).

Leeds
Headingley
Leeds, 1976- 1984
Mother and Baby Home
Diocese
Closed when demand for such homes decreased.

Leeds
St. Anne's
Leeds, 1859- 1895
Parish school / parish visiting
Cathedral parish. A Mass Centre was established from the Cathedral in St. Urban's Parish, where the present convent in Moor Drive is situated.

Leeds
St. Augustine's
Leeds, 1926- 1974
Parish school / parish visiting
Retiring Sister not replaced because of shortage of Sisters. Previously, Sisters

travelled from St. Patrick's 1899 - 1926

Leeds
St. Patrick's
Leeds, 1854- 1990
Five parish schools / parish visiting
Diocesan Catechetical Team
Parish Priest
New convent in York Rd. 1908. Sisters taught in St. Patrick's, St. Charles', St. Brigid's, St. Nicholas' Schools. Catechetics for children in Non-RC schools. 1982 - moved to Old Park Rd. 1990 - moved to Moor Drive, St. Paul's and still continues.

Leeds
St. Paul's, Moor Drive
Leeds, 1990 -
Diocesan Catechetical Team,
Vicar for Religious

Leicester
Evington Hall
Nottingham, 1955-1992
Private primary and (later Diocesan) secondary school / Parish primary school
Congregation of Nativity of BVM, which owned house and school, amalgamated with Sisters of Charity of St. Paul, 1955
House had belonged to the Congregation of the Nativity of the Blessed Virgin Mary. Sisters taught in Sacred Heart Primary School 1968-1970. Sisters withdrew from Secondary School 1977. Junior School closed 1992

Limerick
Bishop's House
Limerick, Ireland, 1979- 1995
Bishop's household: domestic management
Bishop Jeremiah Newman

Kidderminster

Sisters withdrew after the death of Bishop Newman in 1995.

Liverpool
Archbishop's House
Liverpool, 1981- 1996
Archbishop's household: domestic management
Archbishop Worlock
Sisters replaced FCJ Sisters. They helped to look after Pope John Paul II when he stayed in house during his visit to Britain in 1982. Sisters withdrew after the death of Archbishop Worlock in 1996.

Liverpool
Great Mersey St., St. Joseph's
Liverpool, 1908- 1922
Industrial school for boys
The school was attached to St. Joseph's Home for Boys.

Liverpool
Woolton
Liverpool, 1870- 1891
Parish schools / parish visiting
Sisters moved to a larger convent in 1874.

Llanarth
Cardiff, 1887- 1903
Parish schools / parish visiting
catechetics for young women
Father Delerue, p.p.
Sisters took over small school from Sacred Heart Sisters.

Loftus
St. Paul's
Middlesbrough, 1951- 1970
Parish schools: all age, then primary parish visiting

Father Francis Holland p.p.
House in Micklow Lane, then in High St. Closed because of shortage of sisters and availability of Catholic teachers.

Longton
St. Gregory's
Birmingham, 1932-
Parish primary and secondary schools parish visiting
1981. New house in Nashe Drive.

Lydiate
Liverpool, 1857-c1869
Parish school

Macclesfield
Shrewsbury, 1857- ?
Parish school

Maidenhead
St. Paul's
Portsmouth, 1988-
Parish work: catechetical programmes RCIA / Readers' courses
St. Joseph's Parish.

Marlow
Northampton, 1852- 1885
Parish school
Charles Robert Scott-Murray built convent, school, church, presbytery
Early parish logbooks (1852,1854) mention Sisters in "West St., in the house of Robert Clayton."

Marton
St. Ann's
Middlesbrough, c1862-c1870
Parish schools
also called Skirlaugh

Maryport
St.Paul's
Lancaster, 1873-1964
Parish school / parish visiting
Parish Priest (O.S.B.) and Bishop Wilkinson

Middlesbrough
Middlesbrough, c1862-c1867
Parish school

Minsteracres
Hexham & Newcastle, 1976-
Retreat house
Joint Ministry with Passionist Fathers

Modimong
St. Anne's
Rustenburg, South Africa, 1954-1993
Mission schools / hospital / pastoral work / St. Brigid's Sisters
Redemptorists. Mrs Christina Vermaas gave the land
New Diocesan Congregation of Sisters of St. Brigid founded and formed, becoming autonomous in 1987 and taking over from Sisters of St. Paul in 1993.

Mogwase
Holy Family
Rustenburg, South Africa, 1992-1996
Catholic, English - medium primary school
Diocese

Mogwase
Bethany
Rustenburg, South Africa, 1991-
Training College for African Teachers
Diocese
Mankwe Christian College.

Mogwase

Motru
Bucharest, Romania, 1997-
Parish work and school
Archbishop Robu of Bucharest
A donation from the Congregation had already helped to build the church in Motru, when the Archbishop asked in November 1996, for Sisters.

Musselburgh
St. Anne's
Edinburgh, 1907-
Care of elderly / Parish schools
St. Anne's at request of Lady Anne Kerr
Sisters taught in Parish senior and infant schools until 1948. 1986 opening of modern extension of St Anne's Home.

Neston
Shrewsbury, c1861-c1861
Parish schools

Newcastle
St. Andrew's
Hexham & Newcastle, 1881- 1942
Parish schools / parish visiting
Bishop Wilkinson, Hexham and Newcastle
Quayside area - children of labourers. Children came by train for higher education. 1939 evacuation - many children from Nazareth House never returned. Families moved to new estates, Army took over school, later demolished with convent.

Newcastle, Denton Burn
St. Bede's
Hexham & Newcastle, 1942- 1993
Parish school / parish visiting
Sisters travelled from St. Andrew's, Newcastle from 1939. After the war

families moved out to new estates and convent opened near school.

Oakamoor
St. Teresa's
Birmingham, 1903- 1955
Parish school / parish visiting
Diocese
Also known as Cotton. Sisters withdrawn in 1955 because numbers of children fell and Sisters needed elswhere.

Oldbury
George Simmons House
Birmingham, 1986-1993
Sheltered accommodation for the elderly

Oswestry
Our Lady and St. Oswald
Shrewsbury, 1890-
Parish school / parish visiting
Longueville family built convent, school, church and presbytery

Ottawa
St. George's Home
Ottawa, 1907- 1935
Child Care: A receiving house for emigrant boys
Father Hudson's Homes
Closed when Canadian authorities restricted immigration, beacause there was less work available.

Parkstone
St. Paul's
Plymouth, 1931- 1994
Parish AMDG and primary schools / private school.
Fr Michael Coughlan, p.p.
Also called Branksome. 1931 AMDG and Private Schools opened. Latter closed 1962. AMDG became St. Joseph's

Primary. Convents at Alexandra Rd., Penn Hill, St. Aldhelm's Rd.

Penketh
St. Joseph's
Liverpool, 1924-
AMDG and Parish schools / private school / parish work.
1924 Fr. Richard Carr, p.p. (Rainhill). 1996, Request for parish work from local deanery priests and diocese
Opened 1924. Sisters taught in hut next to church, but withdrawn 1927 to enable priest to live in presbytery. Convent opened 1934 at Great Sankey with small private school. 1952 AMDG School . Both became new Parish school 1963. New convent at Larch Ave., Penketh, 1965. Closed 1996 and sisters moved to archdiocesan house, Westbrook, Warrington - parish work .

Phokeng
Rustenburg, South Africa, 1980- 1990
Teaching in local schools and project to teach basic skills
Mgr. Hallett, Prefect Apostolic of Rustenburg
Funding from many businesses. Project handed over to Diocese and Government in 1990.

Prescot
Liverpool, 1859-c1863
Parish school
Bishop Alexander Goss of Liverpool. Later, Sister visits area from Rainhill.

Pretoria
Archbishop's House
Pretoria, South Africa, 1977- 1989

Archbishop's household and seminary: domestic management
Archbishop Daniels

Princethorpe
Princethorpe College
Birmingham, 1978-1987
Boys' independent school - Joint ministry
Sacred Heart Fathers
Sisters withdrawn because of shortage of Sisters.

Radford
St. Mary's
Birmingham, 1854- 1962
Orphanage then boarding school
1834, Miss Bowden gave money for school and house; for two sisters,1854 Miss Bowden was sister to Dr. Bowden, Sedgely Park. Orphanage from 1859 for fifty years (until Rescue Society founded) funded by a priest's bequest, then supported from Banbury. Then boarding school and important branch house. Many sisters buried here. Also served school at Heythrop 1853 - 4.

Rainhill
St. Mary's
Liverpool, 1856-
Parish schools / private school / parish visiting / hospital chaplaincy
Bishop Goss (Liverpool) Bretherton family built school.Parish House Private School closed 1957. New Primary School, St. Bartholomew's, 1962. Last Sister headteacher - 1996. Sisters continue parish and hospital work. Oldest branch house at present (1997) Sisters travelled to teach in Sutton Manor until 1923.

Ripon
St. Wilfrid's
Leeds, 1887- 1989
Parish school / parish visiting
Canon Gordon, p.p. Canon Vavasour built school and church Convent moved four times! Canon Vavasour from the family at Hazlewood Castle.

Rustenburg
Selly Park Convent
Rustenburg, South Africa, 1963-
Schools / parish and catechetical work in surrounding area
Redemptorists. (Replaced Dominican primary school.)
Primary and Secondary Boarding Schools becoming 1983 Day Primary and Pre-School (multiracial). Sisters work in Boitekong (Nursery) and Bapong (Secondary). Now main Convent for Sisters of Charity of St. Paul in South Africa.

Seaham Harbour
St. Francis of Sales
Hexham & Newcastle, c1879- 1886
Parish school

Selby
St. Mary's
Leeds, c1861-1954
Parish schools / parish visiting / Night and Sunday schools
Earlier convent possibly St. Germaine's. Probably closed 1875. Re-opened 1904.

Shefford
St. Francis
Northampton, 1919- 1944
Child Care
Northampton Diocese
Home for boys aged from five to fourteen. Another Congregation took over.

Shipley
Leeds, c1878-c1879
Parish school

Shrewsbury
Bishop's Household
Shrewsbury, 1970-
Bishop's household: domestic management
Bishop Gray
Transferred from Wigan and subsequently to Birkenhead.

South Shields
Hexham & Newcastle, 1982- 1989
Child Care: Family Home
Diocese

Southport
St. Marie's
Liverpool, 1859-
Parish school (until 1977) / parish visiting / Sisters' rest and recuperation
Bishop Alexander Goss (Liverpool)

Southport
St. Patrick's
Liverpool, 1977-
Parish school / parish visiting
Last sister in school withdrawn 1995. Sisters travelled from St. Marie's initially.

Spetchley
Birmingham, 1857- 1863
Parish school: St. Anne's
The Berkely family of Spetchley Park School and convent probably part of Spetchley Park estate. Only about a quarter of the pupils were Catholic. The Elgar family lived near in the 1860's

Standish
St. Teresa's

Standish

Liverpool, 1928- 1963
Parish school / parish visiting
First convent closed 1950. Strickland
House new convent 1950 - 1961 Sisters
travelled from Billinge, later from
Brownedge, when houses closed.

Stanley
St. Joseph's
Hexham & Newcastle, 1908- 1910
Parish school / parish visiting

Stockton on Tees
St. Mary's
Hexham & Newcastle, 1872-1987
*Parish primary and secondary schools
parish visiting*
Bishop Wilkinson - Canon
Carlisle,p.p.
Convent was old mission house on the
quayside, later in Major St. and
Wellington House. Sisters left 1987 and
convent became a hospice. Initially a sea-
faring and ship-building town.

Stourbridge
St. Joseph's
Birmingham, 1872-
*Parish school (until 1992)/ private
school / parish visiting / hospital
chaplaincy*
Mr. Askew built house for the Sisters
Sisters later travelled to Kidderminster
school (1978 - 1988) and Brierley Hill
School (1970 - 1982, 1987 - 1993).
Private School closed 1950. Convent
moved to new house 1977.

Studley
St. Mary's
Birmingham, 1881- 1960
Parish schools / parish visiting
Throckmorton family of Coughton Court

built churches, supported Sisters
Sunbury

St. Teresa's
Westminster, 1926- 1988
*Parish primary school / private school
(later diocesan secondary)*
Private School became Comprehensive,
then amalgamated with boys' school and
Sisters withdrew 1988.

Sutton Coldfield
St. Paul's
Birmingham, 1925-
*Parish school (until 1969) / private
school*
Sisters started small two-roomed school,
St. Joseph's, then new Parish School.
Sisters withdrew 1969. Longest resident:
Miss Nora Conroy from age 17. She died
in 1990. Sisters also taught in Holy Cross
Parish School until 1981.

Sutton Manor
St. Teresa's
Liverpool, 1923 - 1980
Parish school / parish visiting
House closed in 1980 because of shortage
of Sisters. Sisters travelled initially from
Rainhill for school and visiting.

Taunton
Clifton, 1919- 1920
Parish school
Closed in 1920 "small numbers and little
scope."

Teddington
St. Paul's
Westminster, 1884 -
*Parish school / private school / parish
visiting / Juniorate / Retreat house*
Father Akers, p.p.. requested sisters,

1883, before he had any buildings
Also known as Hampton Wick. All - age
school until 1960, then primary. Private
school closed 1961, used as House of
Study for young professed and overseas
Sisters. 1980 became retreat house. 1995
new house, No. 248, for school/parish
Sisters.

Thorndon
Our Lady's
Brentwood, 1868-1901
Parish school / parish visiting
"Lady Petre's Schools" one of the
Jerningham family of Costessey
Thorndon Hall is at Ingrave, Essex. Lady
Petre was widowed, joined Sisters of
Notre Dame and founded Mount
Pleasant College.

Tirgoviste
Bucharest, Romania, 1997-
Parish work and school
Archbishop Robu of Bucharest
One of the first novices in Romania is
from this parish.

Wakefield
St. Joseph's
Leeds, 1858- 1957
*Parish schools / parish and prison
visiting*
1990 return requested by Bishop and
Canon Barr, p.p.
First convent in Teall St (now the
market). New convent , St. Paul's,
opened for parish work 1990 -1995. St.
Austin's Parish.

Walsall
St. Patrick's
Birmingham, 1853-1978
Parish schools / parish visiting

Stanley

First convent 1853 - 1862. Second convent opened 1927. For four years a Sister travelled to school in Shelfield.. Closed 1978 and Sisters travelled from Sutton Coldfield until 1985.

Warrington
Sacred Heart
Liverpool, 1982-
Parish work / hospital chaplaincy
Archdiocese
No resident parish priest. Sisters live in presbytery.

Wednesbury
St. Mary's
Birmingham, 1930- 1959
Parish school / private school / parish visiting
Parish Priest
Sisters took over from FCJ Sisters.

West Bromwich
Birmingham, c1850-c1853
Parish school

Westminster
Archbishop's House
Westminster, 1944- 1957
Archbishop's household: domestic management
Archbishop (later Cardinal) Griffin

Whitehaven
St. Anne's
Lancaster, 1870-1996
Parish schools / parish visiting / Pupil Training Centre (early 19c)
Bishop Wilkinson. Parish Priest (OSB)
Convent next to presbytery, then 3, Corkickle, then Coach Rd after short closure in 1988. During 1912 strike, 500

children given breakfast and dinner for six days.

Whitwick
Holy Cross
Nottingham, 1880- 1888
Parish schools in Gracedieu and Whitwick
Rosminian Sisters before and after Sisters of Charity of St. Paul.

Wimborne
St. Cuthberga's
Plymouth, 1930- 1971
Private school
Later a Sister travelled from Poole to the new Parish primary school.

Worcester
St. George's
Birmingham, 1874- 1984
Parish school / private school / parish visiting
Parish Priest.
First convent at Sansome Place. Later moved to Wyld's Lane. Closed because of shortage of sisters.

Workington
St. Michael's
Lancaster, 1876-
Parish primary schools / secondary school / parish visiting
Bishop Wilkinson. Parish Priest (O.S.B.)
Sisters in St. Michael's and St. Gregory's Primary Schools and in St. Joseph's Secondary School. Convent moved from Banklands to Dupuis House in Stainburn, 1992.

York
St. Wilfrid's
Middlesbrough, 1874- 1994

Parish primary schools / secondary school / parish visiting / catechetics at RAF Station.
First convent a cottage near hospital. Then moved to Monkgate and then to Heworth Green. St. Wilfrid's and St. Aelred's Primary Schools and Margaret Clitherow Secondary School.

Zeerust
St. Mary's
Rustenburg, South Africa, 1954-70
Mission school / pastoral work in surrounding area
Redemptorists
First convent for Sisters in South Africa.

Zeerust

Sisters of Charity of St. Paul the Apostle
Birthplaces of Finally Professed Sisters

1. This list does not include those who left the Congregation during Formation or while under temporary vows. Nor does it include those who left after Final Profession.

2. "Birthplace" does not necessarily indicate nationality.

Years	Great Britain				Ireland			Other	Total
	England	Wales	Scotland	Total	Eire	N.I.	Total		
1847 - 1897	266	2	7	275	249	16	265	8	
1898 - 1947	170	2	18	190	498	20	518	2	
1948 - 1997	62	0	4	66	90	1	91	7	
	498	4	29	531	837	37	874	**17**	1422

Number of Sisters in Congregation 1847 - 1997

Number of Sisters in Congregation 1847 - 1997

Year	No.	Year	No.	Year	No.	Year	No.	Year	No.	Year	No.
1847	2	1872	159	1897	426	1922	577	1947	687	1972	571
1848	3	1873	169	1898	436	1923	575	1948	681	1973	561
1849	4	1874	186	1899	441	1924	594	1949	683	1974	545
1850	6	1875	201	1900	448	1925	597	1950	681	1975	534
1851	11	1876	229	1901	454	1926	607	1951	678	1976	519
1852	16	1877	241	1902	466	1927	612	1952	677	1977	508
1853	24	1878	268	1903	474	1928	628	1953	678	1978	499
1854	33	1879	291	1904	487	1929	639	1954	674	1979	498
1855	39	1880	304	1905	499	1930	644	1955	683	1980	491
1856	46	1881	314	1906	508	1931	647	1956	679	1981	478
1857	62	1882	317	1907	517	1932	667	1957	685	1982	474
1858	74	1883	332	1908	524	1933	682	1958	675	1983	458
1859	78	1884	342	1909	535	1934	687	1959	670	1984	446
1860	91	1885	356	1910	551	1935	687	1960	668	1985	438
1861	102	1886	370	1911	549	1936	693	1961	665	1986	426
1862	115	1887	382	1912	553	1937	702	1962	651	1987	420
1863	117	1888	387	1913	561	1938	708	1963	640	1988	405
1864	118	1889	390	1914	572	1939	699	1964	640	1989	398
1865	123	1890	392	1915	573	1940	700	1965	636	1990	389
1866	124	1891	396	1916	578	1941	698	1966	625	1991	380
1867	129	1892	397	1917	574	1942	688	1967	614	1992	373
1868	133	1893	405	1918	578	1943	689	1968	611	1993	361
1869	140	1894	412	1919	577	1944	685	1969	605	1994	350
1870	141	1895	413	1920	577	1945	687	1970	591	1995	345
1871	153	1896	420	1921	577	1946	691	1971	582	1996	338
										1997	324

Sisters of Charity of St. Paul the Apostle

Age Structure in January 1995

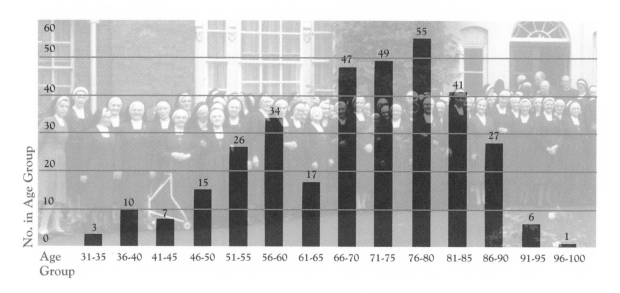

Sisters not interred at Selly Park

Place	Name	Dates
Ashton in Makerfield	Sr. Genevieve Marie O'Shea	1875-1946
	Sr. Marie Canice Maher	1885-1960
Banbury	Sr. M. Francisca Morten	1831-1900
	Sr. M. Genevieve Teresa Cook	1862-1908
	Sr. M. Agnes Rose Doherty	1895-1969
Batley	Sr. Madeline des Anges Thompson	1857-1890
	Sr. M. St. Agnes O'Grady	1860-1926
	Sr. Marie Bonaventure Butler	1877-1937
	Sr. M. Teresa Gertrude Ryder	1879-1962
	Sr. M. Anthony Josephine Carey	1890-1968
	Sr. M. St. Chad Noonan	1888-1970
Birstall	Sr. Mary of the Cross Hutchinson	1869-1933
	Sr. Francis Mary O'Connor	1858-1934
	Sr. M. Agnes Josephine Dunne	1887-1961
Bishop Thornton	Sr. M. Pauline Kavaney	1834-1893
Boston	Sr. M. St. Teresa Netterville	1845-1924
Bradford	Sr. M. Jane Francis Grimshaw	1827-1865
	Sr. M. Pius McGarry	1836-1865
	Sr. Rose of the Cross Coleman	1861-1933
	Sr. Madeleine of St. Joseph Conway	1826-1941
	Sr. Paul de Marie Feeney	1880-1941
	Sr. M. Patricia Kevin Lonergan	1895-1972
Brewood	Sr. M. Stephanie Coughlan	1829-1862
Broadway	Sr. Marie Finbarr Lynch	1891-1918
Brooms	Sr. St. Madeline Wright	1843-1911
	Sr. M. Imelda Turner	1840-1914
	Sr. St. Thecla Murphy	1851-1914
	Sr. Aloysia MacDonald	1864-1932
	Sr. Agnes Gertrude Curtin	1887-1938
	Sr. Albertine of Mary Bradley	1882-1945
Brownedge	Sr. Benedict Joseph Merritt	1846-1867
	Sr. M. Petronilla Rafter	1840-1868
	Sr. M. Stanislaus Connolly	1836-1876

Brownedge	Sr. St. Anne Buckley	1849-1898
	Sr. Agnes Josephine Foley	1865-1908
	Sr. M. Catherine Joseph Morrissey	1892-1917
	Sr. M. Thèrèse Joseph Gregson	1859-1938
	Sr. Mary of Perpetual Help Delaney	1862-1943
	Sr. M. Francis of five Wounds Dalton	1891-1958
Buckfast	Sr. M. Cecilia Dunne	1865-1940
Cheltenham	Sr. M. Magdalen Thompson	1821-1881
	Sr. M. Casimir Boardman	1835-1904
Crook	Sr. Marie de L'Enfant Jèsu Duffy	1859-1881
	Sr. Teresa Clare Casey	1859-1897
	Sr. M. Praxedes Flusk	1837-1904
Crosby	Sr. M. John Chrysostom Nolan	1851-1912
	Sr. Augustine Marie Grace	1872-1938
	Sr. M. Seraphina of St. Thèrèse Rush	1911-1960
Darlington	Sr. M. St. Agathe Cashin	1876-1931
	Sr. St. Blandina Bolger	1865-1938
Dipton	Sr. M. Lorenzo Brophy	1886-1976
Dublin	Sr. St. Benedict Tolan	1856-1889
	Sr. John Berchmans Foran	1883-1945
Dudley	Sr. M. Margaret Goulding	1828-1865
	Sr. M. Aemilian Bradley	1837-1871
	Sr. Katherina Marie Scollen	1860-1904
Edinburgh	Sr. Josephina Mary Kelly	1858-1922
	Sr. Marie Michel Whitwell	1857-1922
	Sr. M. St. Clotilda Connolly	1874-1953
Esh Laude	Sr. Magdalen of Jesus Croake	1858-1924
	Sr. M. Vincent Gerard Woods	1889-1954
Exton	Sr. M. Françoise de Sales O'Brien	1872-1898
	Sr. Berchmans Marie Kennedy	1891-1918
Formby	Sr. Bernard of Mary Whittle	1862-1939
Garstang	Sr. M. Jane Berchmans Dunne	1865-1911
	Sr. Francis Benedict Dalton	1882-1949

Glossop	Sr. M. Beatrice Morris	1867-1899
	Sr. M. St. Angela Padbury	1864-1900
	Sr. M. de Sales Rice	1853-1919
	Sr. M. Alphonsus O'Malley	1888-1938
Hawick	Sr. Patricia Marie McNulty	1877-1951
	Sr. M. Victorina Hubberd	1876-1955
	Sr. Paul Mary Noonan	1878-1958
Kendal	Sr. Rose Editha Smith	1867-1917
Kensal Green	Sr. Maria Philomene Denault	1860-1911
Kilfinane	Sr. Marie Brendan Ryder	1887-1938
	Sr. St. Anselm Holmes	1897-1976
	Sr. Magdalen de Pazzi Dwan	1914-1993
	Sr. M. St. Thecla Goggin	1912-1994
Kilmallock	Sr. M. St. Clement Cavanagh	1868-1942
	Sr. M. Borgia Fitzgerald	1881-1955
	Sr. Bernadette Marie Griffiths	1893-1956
	Sr. M. Alphonsus Liguori Comber	1901-1964
	Sr. M. Martina Kennedy	1898-1972
	Sr. M. St. Claude Cahill	1908-1973
	Sr. M. Agnes Xavier McArdle	1900-1974
	Sr. M. St. Mel Connery	1903-1981
	Sr. M. St. Celsus O'Riordan	1899-1986
	Sr. Máire M. Lyons	1942-1993
Leamington	Sr. M. of Presentation McMahon	1841-1912
Leeds	Sr. M. Germaine Briscoe	1840-1885
	Sr. M. Teresa of Sacred Heart O'Hare	1862-1899
	Sr. M. Malachy Nolan	1864-1911
	Sr. M. Sebastian Mordaunt	1879-1912
	Sr. M St. Ursula Cunningham	1895-1957
	Sr. Maris Stella Brennan	1876-1966
Llanarth	Sr. M. Priscilla Ainsworth	1831-1894
Marlow	Sr. M. Patricia Connolly	1839-1863
Maryport	Sr. M. Patricia Josephine McDonnell	1886-1945
	Sr. M. Kieran Kelliher	1887-1955
Modimong	Sr. M. of Mount Carmel Collins	1937-1986

Newcastle	Sr. Marie Augustine Purtle	1845-1890
	Sr. M. Annunciata Kennedy	1840-1898
	Sr. M. Genevieve McGrath	1853-1900
	Sr. M.Isidore Daly	1858-1922
	Sr. Katerina Marie Curtis	1877-1962
	Sr. Marie Aidan Shanley	1909-1979
Oswestry	Sr. M. St. Edward Matthews	1874-1942
	Sr. Ignatius Marie Bruen	1878-1957
Ottawa	Sr. M. Evangelist O'Keeffe	1857-1926
Pantasaph	Sr. M. Prisca O'Donnell	1832-1889
	Sr. M. of the Assumption Savin	1844-1892
	Sr. M. Werberge Bailey	1837-1899
	Sr. Madeline Thompson	1841-1904
	Sr. Basilissia Ahearne	1861-1922
	Sr. Marie Madelina of B.S. Clay	1858-1927
	Sr. St. Catherine of Sienna Lyndon	1853-1933
Plymouth	Sr. M. Rosaline Sinnott	1876-1936
	Sr. Ita Joseph Nolan	1884-1951
Radford	Sr. M. Catherine Simpson	1829-1855
	Sr. M. Gonzaga Johnson	1837-1857
	Sr. M. Evangelist Johnson	1839-1858
	Sr. M. Rosalie Croskell	1841-1858
	Sr. M. of Presentation Grimshaw	1838-1861
	Sr. Augusta Boyle	1833-1862
	Sr. M. Columba Gahan	1833-1862
	Sr. Maria Windsor	1837-1863
	Sr. M. Josepha Hewitt	1830-1864
	Sr. M. St. John Chopping	1831-1867
	Sr. Francis Borgia McShane	1858-1879
	Sr. M. Francis Borgia Winter	1802-1882
	Sr. M. Angelina Foley	1839-1900
	Sr. M. Barbara Guest	1839-1902
	Sr. Marie Winefride Flynn	1862-1942
	Sr. Nicholas of Seven Dolours O'Keeffe	1884-1946
	Sr. Marie Thérèse Gaffney	1861-1947
Rainhill	Sr. M. Agnes of Assisi O'Malley	1868-1910
	Sr. Joannes O'Donnell	1841-1921
Rochfort Bridge	Sr. Ignatius Marie Rowan	1867-1893

Selby	Sr. M. Placida Foley	1829-1906
Southport	Sr. M. Josephine Canty	1843-1871
	Sr. M. Veronica Heath	1813-1880
	Sr. M. Gerard O'Dwyer	1881-1921
	Sr. M. St. Finbarr Duggan	1891-1965
Stockton	Sr. M. Isidora Chapman	1845-1880
	Sr. M. de St. Charles McDermott	1869-1902
	Sr. Mary Anselm Hughes	1876-1916
Sutton Manor	Sr. Ambrose Marie Curtin	1886-1941
Teddington	Sr. M. Aloysius Berchams Gibbs	1856-1918
	Sr. Marie Victorine Denis	1852-1926
	Sr. M. Angela Minogue	1877-1941
	Sr. M. St. Cecile Battey	1910-1941
	Sr. Magdalene Joseph Cullen	1859-1941
Thorndon	Sr. St. Gertrude Maguire	1840-1893
Wakefield	Sr. Loretto Smith	1844-1881
	Sr. M. Zita Rowe	1826-1893
	Sr. St. Michelle Fauvel	1839-1901
	Sr. M. Agnes Gertrude Gilhooly	1852-1906
	Sr. M. Alphonsus Joseph Grace	1859-1937
Waterford	Sr. M. Marcella Brennan	1852-1922
	Sr. Alphonsus Marie Halpin	1857-1935
	Sr. Agnes Genevieve Fenton	1857-1937
Whitehaven	Sr. M. Hilda Gregson	1835-1905
	Sr. Hilda Francis Appleby	1881-1915
Worcester	Sr. M. Ignatius Carraway	1857-1881
	Sr. Joseph Marie Daley	1847-1886
Workington	Sr. St. Cuthbert Anderson	1856-1907
	Sr. Marie de la Croix O'Keefe	1863-1913
	Sr. M. Eustelle of St. Joseph Whitehead	1866-1918
	Sr. Joseph of the Sacred Heart McArdle	1865-1934
York	Sr. Magdalen Patricia Mordaunt	1867-1936
Unknown	Sr. Gonzague Marie Hackett	1850-1876
	Sr. Marie Vincent Malone	1859-1882

General Chapter, 1992 at Newman College. First Chapter in which all Sisters were invited to participate, except for voting - reserved for elected delegates. Therefore, because about 120 Sisters attended, it was the first Chapter to be held outside Selly Park.